eBu$iness

7 steps to getting your small business online and making money now!

Paul Wallbank

Wrightbooks

First published in 2011 by Wrightbooks
an imprint of John Wiley & Sons Australia, Ltd
42 McDougall St, Milton Qld 4064

Office also in Melbourne

Typeset in 11.3/14 pt Berkeley oldstyle Book

© Paul Wallbank 2011

The moral rights of the author have been asserted

National Library of Australia Cataloguing-in-Publication data:

Author:	Wallbank, Paul.
Title:	eBu$iness: 7 steps to getting your small business online and making money now / Paul Wallbank.
ISBN:	9780730376255 (pbk.)
Notes:	Includes index.
Subjects:	Electronic commerce. Small business—Management. Success in business.
Dewey Number:	381.142

Cover design by Peter Reardon, Pipeline Design <www.pipelinedesign.com.au>

Cover images: © newgeneration, 2011/© Julien Tromeur. Used under license from Shutterstock.com

Printed in Australia by Ligare Book Printer

10 9 8 7 6 5 4 3 2 1

Disclaimer

The material in this publication is of the nature of general comment only, and does not represent professional advice. It is not intended to provide specific guidance for particular circumstances and it should not be relied on as the basis for any decision to take action or not take action on any matter which it covers. Readers should obtain professional advice where appropriate, before making any such decision. To the maximum extent permitted by law, the author and publisher disclaim all responsibility and liability to any person, arising directly or indirectly from any person taking or not taking action based on the information in this publication.

Contents

About the author

Paul Wallbank is one of Australia's leading experts on how businesses and consumers use the web. In 1995 he had the foresight to set up a computer service business, PC Rescue, after discovering that few businesses were providing IT support specifically for home and small businesses. His company quickly grew to cover all of Australia.

Paul is a regular technology expert on ABC radio and a columnist for <www.smartcompany.com.au>. He also runs workshops and consulting services for corporate, government and community groups on a range of topics relating to the rise of digital industries, connected communities and pervasive computing.

Paul has written seven books on internet use, including *The Internet For Dummies*.

Visit Paul at <www.ebusinessbook.com.au> for bonus information and great tips on getting your small business online.

Introduction

At the time of writing *eBusiness* in early 2011, the use of social media has exploded. Facebook has raced past 600 million users; Google has offered US$6 billion to buy daily offer site Groupon; and smart phones are outselling personal computers. The way we do business is rapidly evolving as these technologies change our world.

Many businesses feel challenged by these changes. At the end of 2010 some of the Australian retailing industry tried to turn back the tide with a campaign for tax changes to stop people buying online. These retailers didn't understand that the internet's real effects on their businesses are a lot more subtle and powerful than saving a few GST dollars.

Driving most of the change is how our customers, suppliers and employees are becoming more informed by using the web to discover who we are and talking to each other about their experiences in dealing with us. In this environment, having an online presence becomes a business essential.

In my opinion, there are three reasons why businesses haven't gone online: the cost, the jargon, and the time it takes to set up a website or social media presence. This book will show you how to set up a full web presence in just seven easy steps — it won't take you more than a weekend to implement a basic but functional and professional look.

eBusiness will help anyone who wants to get their ideas, project or business onto the internet cheaply and effectively. Much of the advice here is for small or start-up organisations that want to get their message out to the world.

You can also visit the *eBusiness* website at <www.ebusinessbook. com.au> to find bonus resources such as links, frequently asked questions and advice on web consultants.

Towards the end of writing *eBusiness*, Google and MYOB launched their Getting Australian Businesses Online project, which also helps local merchants set up a website. The appendix includes an overview as well as the instructions to help you maximise your results through this terrific service.

Earlier, I mentioned three reasons for why businesses are not online, but there's also a fourth reason and that is that many businesses think they don't need a website. Those days are over. In a world where our customers, staff and suppliers are online, we have to be online as well. This book will show you how to create an internet presence quickly and effectively so you can grab the opportunities on offer.

Chapter 1

Define your business

Given that most business writing about the internet focuses on marketing, it's tempting to think the internet is just a marketing tool, and nothing more than a glorified electronic brochure or business card. Thinking about the internet that way would be a great mistake, as the web isn't just a means of drawing attention to ourselves. Our customers are looking for us on the internet, and everyone—our suppliers, creditors, debtors, employees—is checking our web profile before doing business with us.

For tradespeople, the move to mobile internet and online directories has meant that customers are logging on to find plumbers, electricians and locksmiths. In most cases, it's easier to find a mobile phone or computer than to find and rummage through a printed phone directory. Today, having some sort of presence on the web is overtaking the traditional advertisement in the local newspaper or phone book as the main way to advertise your services.

When customers go online they not only find our website — and our competitors' sites — but can also see comments on social media and product review sites, where previous clients discuss how good a meal, product or service was. Our reputations are now being set by what other people are saying about us online.

The internet is a great marketing platform, but today your business brand and reputation are more than just a function of what you claim and promote: it's increasingly about how you deliver what you promise.

First, though, we have to make those promises and that's the first reason your business has to be on the web. If your business isn't on the web, then for many people it simply doesn't exist. So what are we trying to do on the Net?

What is your business?

The web can be a pretty brutal place. Social media and review sites will punish anyone — particularly businesses — who misrepresent themselves or don't deliver on their promises. It's important to understand what your business is and what value it adds for customers before you start making grand claims.

While this might sound scary, it is in fact an opportunity for smaller and more nimble organisations to promote themselves. In this era of big business spouting the mantras of shareholder returns and corporate responsibility, it's easy to miss the point that the whole reason a business exists is to deliver a product to the customer.

The major weakness of big businesses is that most workers in large corporations have nothing to do with serving the customer. Instead, they spend their time writing memos and engaging in office politics.

Because your business doesn't have this massive, flabby overhead, you can execute your ideas quickly and comparatively cheaply. And this book aims to help you do just that.

Which markets are you catering to?

It's easy to talk about our market but who the heck are they? Are they other business owners, the local accountant, married retirees, expectant mothers, baby boomers, gen X, gen Y or the younger Millennials?

One assumption that's often proved wrong is that all internet users are young. The reality is that while those in the 25–39 year old age bracket grew up with computers and are high users of technology, older age groups are rapidly catching up. If you sell to seniors, don't assume they aren't online, as they are increasingly joining the connected masses.

We make a lot of assumptions about our customers and we're often proved wrong. Luckily the flexibility and cost of the web means we can test new ideas and change things quickly. Having said that, your existing knowledge does influence the channels you use. If you are selling to other business owners, for instance, it makes sense to invest more in your LinkedIn presence; a maternity shop owner is probably going to be more focused on having a presence on internet baby forums; and a pizza shop might find that Twitter is the best place to advertise daily deals (see figure 1.1, overleaf).

Figure 1.1: Crust pizza Twitter feed

Where do you want to sell?

Some businesses have global ambitions, while others are quite happy to occupy a corner in their neighbourhood. Each extreme needs a web presence, but the needs of the aspiring multinational are quite different from those of local businesses.

One challenge for big, established businesses is the growth of online stores and payment systems, but not every organisation needs or wants to be selling online. What a business chooses to do regarding e-commerce will determine how great their online needs are.

Later chapters will look at the various options and which ones are useful for different types of business. It's important to keep in mind that running a business is a journey—plans change and new opportunities come along—so throughout the book we're looking at the most flexible options for an online presence—ones that can grow and adapt with the changing needs of your venture.

What do you want from the Net?

When we make an investment decision the question is how does the investment meet our business objectives? Every internet decision is an outlay of either our time or our money, and time is the much scarcer and more valuable asset for a business owner.

To define what we are looking for from the internet, we can boil down some key objectives for most businesses.

Marketing

The most common use companies make of the Net is marketing and it's true that the internet—in fact anything to do with computers—is the greatest marketing tool ever invented for small business.

In print and older media the idea of marketing was to shout at people through advertising. The more a company could afford in big newspaper ads, billboards and loud, obnoxious radio and TV ads the better.

In the online era those methods still work, but things have changed subtly. Today we don't have to shout, as the audience can filter us out or use channels, such as search engines like Google, that don't work well as a platform for shouting. If we use online marketing, we still need to spend time and money, but we don't have to shout or go big. We'll look at some of the specific marketing strategies later, but we need to understand at the beginning of the process exactly how we're going to use online tools.

Getting out the message that we are open for business — that we are the best hairdresser in Toowoomba, the best plumber in Northbridge or the best baker in Launceston — is the basic function that all businesses need from the web.

Marketing is the basic, but not the only, purpose of an online presence, and it's a mistake to focus just on the marketing aspects of a website. The web is much more than just telling the world your opening hours and which credit cards you accept.

Recruitment

The internet has taken over as the main way to recruit staff. Most job advertisements have moved from newspapers onto the web and now the social media platforms, such as Facebook and LinkedIn, are becoming the main way for businesses to find staff.

Prospective employees are also checking out your site to see what jobs are available, what sort of business you are and who your best contacts are. Having a presentable website means you can tell people who you are and what you do.

When people do find a job that looks good, they log in and look up details of the employer on the web, Facebook and LinkedIn to see what the organisation is like and who they know there.

If your intention is to find the right people online, you will need to have a presence that encourages applicants to find you and send you their details. In many industries, particularly hospitality, lots of negative or aggressive comments on review sites or social media can turn potential employees off as they begin to sense there is a problem with the business or they will have to deal with stroppy customers. When dealing with negativity online, business owners and managers win fans with sensible, considered and empathetic responses. By coming across as a level-headed person, you not only win customers but also show prospective staff that you're someone reasonable to work for.

Suppliers

In all businesses, one of the recurring questions is 'Can I trust this guy to pay me?' So the more information you can give to your potential creditors the better. A consistent web presence assures those you ask for credit that you are a viable organisation that can be trusted to pay its bills.

Authorities

Even the biggest free-market capitalists find themselves having to deal with government, even if it's only to prove to the Tax Office that their business is legitimate. A web presence gives the bureaucrats evidence that you are a legitimate, operating business. That legitimacy also counts if you find yourself in a trademark dispute, as an internet presence proves you have been trading under a name for some time.

In recent times it's been popular to talk about a business's USP—unique selling proposition—as the key difference between enterprises. The USP idea, however, looks at only one aspect of how every business is different.

A business is a human, social enterprise made up of individuals: the owner, staff, customers and suppliers all impose their unique personalities on the business and make it what it is. Even when the objectives of two businesses are the same, each one will follow different paths to achieve them. The same is true on the Net: each of us has a different way of using the web, and we have to acknowledge those differences—what works online for one business won't necessarily work for the competitor down the road.

Listening and learning

The web is a great place for listening and learning—in many ways it's a free market research tool. One of the great advantages for small and new businesses is the online social media channels. Blogs and forums let us listen in to what the market is saying about us and our competitors.

It also gives us a window to the world: we can read about the latest trends in New York, Tokyo, London, Shanghai or Paris as they are happening. What would once have taken weeks or months to filter its way through magazines and newspapers is now on your desktop as it happens. This gives smaller, more flexible businesses a massive advantage over the larger, more slow-moving organisations. It means you can be ahead of the market and bigger competitors. This listening advantage for small business is grossly understated, as the Net is one of the most valuable listening tools we have.

Thought leadership

Many people own a business because that's where they work best. Often these folk are original thinkers, which is why they don't work well in bigger, bureaucratic organisations. One of the advantages the Net offers this group is that it provides a publishing platform that gives you the opportunity to become a leader in your industry or community.

The web offers a great opportunity to get your ideas into the marketplace, which can establish you and your business as leaders. A good example of this is the Australian News-agency blog (see figure 1.2) where the owner, Mark Fletcher, has established himself as a leader in the industry, which helps grow his retail software business.

Figure 1.2: Australian Newsagency blog

Budgets

Just as the reach of the web is huge, so too are website budgets. Some big organisations spend tens, sometimes hundreds, of millions of dollars in building their web presence. Often their massive expenditure fails as they still think in terms of shouting across a hundred markets that they make the funkiest jeans, blingiest shoes or most refreshing drink.

While shouting can work, it generally fails online because people can just flick to another website or stop following you on Facebook and Twitter. So the web changes some of the fundamental ideas of modern marketing. This opens a wonderful opportunity for small business owners, who may not have the budgets, but are closer to their markets and have a better feeling for what customers want.

We should take care not to forget there are costs to using the web even with 'free' services: it will cost you something in either time or money. While this book looks at doing things cheaply, we shouldn't forget that well-spent money will take your online presence a lot further. We will look more closely at some of the costs involved in setting up a web presence, and where smaller and cash-strapped businesses can defray or delay some of their costs until they have more money in the bank.

How do you sell?

Your online presence is also going to be affected by how your online sales channels work. You may find that a poorly worded website or Facebook page will get you flooded with enquiries you can't deal with. Make sure you have considered how you're going to project your presence online to avoid disappointing customers or, even worse, being overwhelmed by work you can't handle.

Timelines and business plans

Naturally everything has to fit into your business plan and timelines. There's no point in launching a website before you've decided on a business or product name, for instance. It's also counter-productive to have a local listing or an active social media presence before you have opened your store. The online and the physical worlds are deeply related and work together: we can't ignore one or the other.

Credibility: the 360 degree brand

All of the examples discussed in this book show that today everyone you deal with is using the internet to check out your business. Probably the biggest thing the internet has done is break down the idea that marketing and branding are separate from other business aspects. If you are a bad payer or lousy employer, people are going to be talking about that online. If you are providing great service, people will also be talking about that.

By not being found online, you're creating a vacuum and the internet loves filling empty spaces, often with misinformation. If your website is the first thing web-surfers see when they are online, you fill that hole and give people a place to gather around you.

Conclusion

Everything you do on the Net has effects in the offline world, so a well-planned internet presence works to unite the various messages. Having a basic web setup is important just to let the world know who you are, and the good news is that many of the important tools, such as listing with the key online directories, are free. Step 1 will look establishing an online presence using free tools, such as free listing sites and how to go about adding your details to useful sites.

Checklist

> If you're launching a new business, have you included websites in your business plan?

> Who are the people you want to attract to your business?

> Can you sum up your business in 140 characters?

> Are you planning to sell online?

> Do you intend to sell overseas?

> What are your budgets?

> How long are the timelines you are looking at?

Step 1

The free web tools

Chapter 2

Local directories

Of all the chapters in this book, this one is probably both the simplest and the most vital, which is why I have put it at the front. While website design, domain names, payment systems and social media are important, the basic search engine listings are the foundations of an internet presence.

Amazingly these really important services are free and it takes only a few minutes' work to enter the relevant details. In fact getting your information into all seven of the key services discussed here shouldn't take more than three hours to complete, subject to your having all the key information at hand.

Along with putting your business in the search engines and local business sites, a listing will also feed into other directories, the social media platforms and even global positioning systems, which have started offering features like searches for hotels, cafes and service stations into their mapping software.

Today the search engine is the basis of most internet use; even services that technically aren't part of the world wide web (for instance iPhone apps) still rely on data that they have found on the web. So the listing of your sites in these services is possibly the most important thing you can do when setting up your online presence.

Search engine submissions

The search engines will eventually find you, but you can speed the process up by telling them you are on the internet and open for business. In the early days of the web, sites such as Yahoo! planned to charge for these listings, but Google's arrival put paid to those ideas, and today a basic listing with all the search engines is free, though they still offer some priority paid options.

Google listing

As an organisation that genuinely loves data, Google gives businesses and individuals a whole range of opportunities to list websites, businesses, video clips and many other online services, which they describe in their *Submit your content* page (visit the *eBusiness* website at <www.ebusinessbook. com.au> for the link). Figure 2.1 shows the page where you can add your information.

Of all the submission services Google offers, the two most important are Google Places and *Add your URL*. I will look at Google Places later. Adding your business's URL (universal resource locator)—a geeky way of saying web address—to Google's index is quick and straightforward.

Figure 2.1: Google's submit your content page

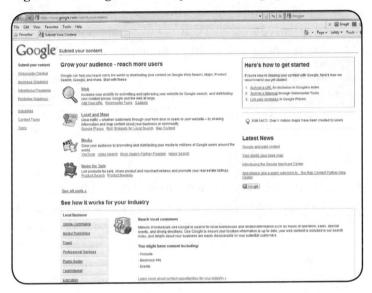

Visit the Google *Add your URL* page at <www.google.com/addurl> and fill in the website address—don't forget to put the http:// in front of the rest of the address—then fill in a brief description of your site (see figure 2.2).

Figure 2.2: add your URL to Google

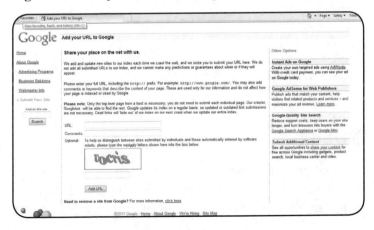

While Google claims the description won't affect your page's search ranking, it's worthwhile putting in a concise description of your site. Then complete the CAPTCHA to show that you're a real human being and not an evil spambot.

Your site will now come to the attention of Google's software robots (known as crawlers or spiders) which find websites and index what they contain. Click 'Add URL' and you're finished.

Microsoft Bing

The new kid on the block among the big boys is Microsoft Bing. As part of the world's biggest software company, this search engine is turned on automatically on most computers. So it is worth taking the five minutes to sign in to Bing and register your site. The process is even easier than Google's (see figure 2.3).

Figure 2.3: submit your site to Bing

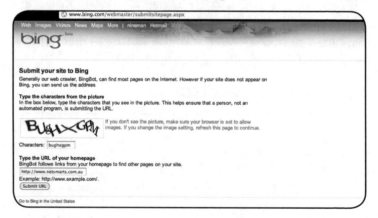

Yahoo!

Coming up third, but still important, is Yahoo!, which dominated the web until Google came along. Despite Yahoo!'s steady decline in relevance, it is still an important place to list your site, which you can do by visiting <http://siteexplorer .search.yahoo.com>. The layout of Yahoo!'s submission page is even more spartan than Bing's (see figure 2.4), which makes it quick to fill in, if nothing else.

Figure 2.4: Yahoo! site explorer

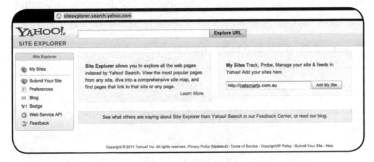

Local business centre listings

The real battlefield for search engines at the moment is in local listings. As consumers move from using local newspaper classifieds and printed phone directories to online services, the search engines are positioning themselves to deliver better information to people searching for shops, trades and services in their neighbourhoods.

Small businesses are the winner in this battle, as the big search engine companies are making it easier for local merchants to list, and they are also offering very comprehensive and easy-to-use products. The big two in Australia are News Limited's True Local and Google Places.

Google Local Business

Google reigns supreme in local business as it does for the rest of web, as it feeds into almost every other service, as well as being the dominant search engine in almost every market. Getting your Google listing correct is the first, important step.

The Google Local Business Centre underlies many of Google's mobile and other listing services, and it also fits into the popular Google Maps application (see figure 2.5). Every business should be on this already as the listing is free and the information also feeds into Google search results.

Figure 2.5: Google Maps search

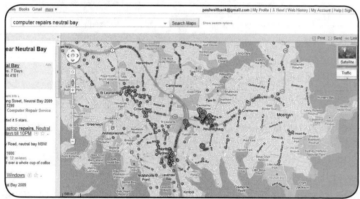

If your organisation is correctly listed on Google Local Business, it will appear in all Google searches for your product in your neighbourhood. It's a great example of how local businesses, from plumbers to hairdressers, can make things work for themselves.

Even more importantly, the search results plug into many of the other local and social media services such as Foursquare and Twitter that we'll discuss later in the chapter. So by listing in Google your business gets coverage on many other outlets across the internet.

If you already have a website, checking if you are already listed is easy. Go to the Google Local site at <www.google .com/local> and type in the name of your business. There's a very good chance it will show up, as Google takes in listing information from other services, such as the Yellow Pages and social media sites. If your place is listed, click on the 'Business owner?' link and you will be taken to a series of choices, such as 'Edit my business information', 'Suspend this listing' or 'This isn't my listing' (see figure 2.6).

Figure 2.6: claiming a Google Local listing

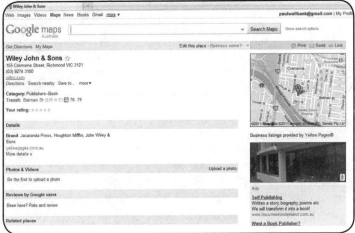

Assuming this is your business, you can then enter the site and go through the details available. Answer the questions in a way that portrays your business in the best possible light and don't forget to add the words that customers use when looking for your products or services. We look at keywords (the terms people search for) later in the chapter.

In the Google Places listing (see figure 2.7, overleaf), ensure that all your contact details, addresses, opening hours and payment details are correct. The important thing is to fill in as many boxes as you can and, where possible, add as much description as possible about your products and services, as this is what customers are looking for.

Figure 2.7: Google Places listing page

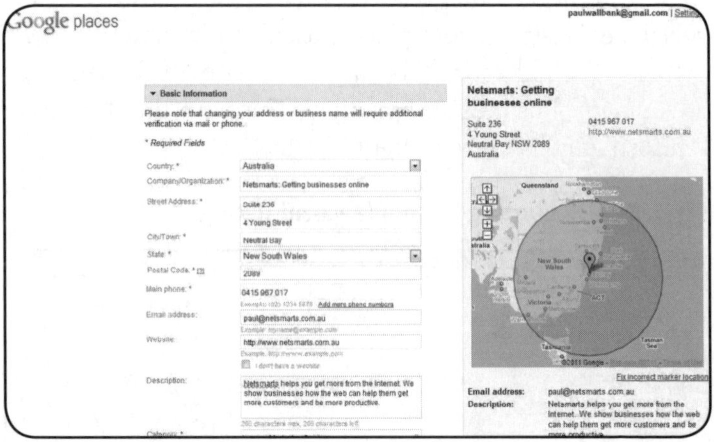

Coupon power

One of the things Google and the other local business platforms love is discount coupons. Both Google Places and True Local have sections that allow you to enter offers and deals, which will improve your rankings in the local directories.

It's a great idea to do this regularly, adding, say, 'buy one, get one free' or '10 per cent off new water heaters' offers. If you have a free ebook, complimentary coffee or bands performing, you can add those: you don't have to include discounts with the offer.

While the term coupon implies they have to be printed pieces of paper, and the way Google and True Local lay them out makes them look like those you would clip out of a magazine, you don't have to insist customers print them out to redeem them. You can use whatever method you like to validate and monitor what your customers do with your offers.

The coupon industry is taking off and there's no reason why you shouldn't add your own offers. Look at being creative and treat them as another way to publicise your business.

Another trick is to cross-reference services in the 'Extras' fields at the bottom of the listing page. You can add custom fields to your site, such as listing your business's Facebook and Twitter accounts (see chapter 3).

Choosing keywords and file names

When filling in your details, remember that keywords matter and what you put into the descriptions will be indexed by Google. Make sure you include keywords that you think customers will search for when looking for a business like yours (see step 5 for more information).

The webmaster tools that allow you to track online progress have features that help you figure out which are the popular words driving customers to your site (see step 4 for more information).

It's also a good idea to put yourself in the position of the customer to ensure you include all the keywords a customer might use in a search. What does the customer look for when they are searching for your business? Those terms, like coffee if you run a café, are the things people will type into the search engines.

The keywords should also be reflected in the extras you upload, so that any photos, videos or other information should include those keywords. On Google Places, you can upload up to 10 images, so include five that are popular items and another five that are high-margin goods or lines that you want to move. For instance, if you're a plumber specialising in hot water systems, you might want to upload some pictures or videos of work being done on a hot water system with file names such as 'Hot water system repair' or 'Hot water tank replacement'.

Naming a file

One of the things search engines love is descriptive names of things like video clips and photos, so take some time in naming the files before you upload them to the website.

In the case of a plumber offering hot water services, they may name a picture showing the product, 'Installation of hot water service by a qualified local plumber'. This is the sort of name that the search engines will index when searching the site, making it more likely that someone searching for a plumber to install a water heater is going to find you.

When naming files, don't be too descriptive as you may get penalised by the search engines for being spammy. A good description summarises what the file is and its relevance to your web page.

Try to keep your file sizes below 100K as anything bigger starts to slow the website down. Surveys show that slower sites are less competitive.

Some other aspects of adding this basic information to search engines, such as 'alt text', can improve page loading times, as well as enhance the search engine's efficiency in finding your site. See step 5 for more in-depth information on search engine optimisation.

As well as loading images and videos, you should link your website with any Facebook, YouTube or other accounts. We'll look at those services, which are also free, in chapter 3. The idea is to use as many of these channels as possible to improve your site's visibility online.

Everything you do in Google Local, as well as with competitors such as True Local and Microsoft's Bing Local Listings, can be changed later, so don't worry if you intend to launch a new product or update branding later down the track.

Having spent half an hour setting up your service, keeping it refreshed and current with new offers, rotating pictures or altering custom fields adds a lot of credibility in the eyes of Google and will keep your business at the top of the listing.

The Google verification process

At the end of the Google Pages process, you'll be asked to verify your ownership. Depending upon the contact details you've filled in, you'll be given the choice of confirming by phone, SMS or post. The confirmation will include a personal information number (PIN), which you enter into your listing to confirm ownership.

True Local

News Limited's True Local service (see figure 2.8, overleaf) acts in a similar way to Google's Local Business Centre and has the benefit of feeding into News Limited's local newspaper network, the Yahoo!7 services and Navman GPS. It's a fairly comprehensive range of online networks and it shouldn't be ignored, because it has great strategic marketing value.

The signup process is similar to Google's and takes about the same amount of time. Some people find that, after signing into True Local, they receive some sales calls from the media and advertising arms of News Limited and their advertising partners, but that's a very small price to pay for the free listing.

Figure 2.8: True Local homepage

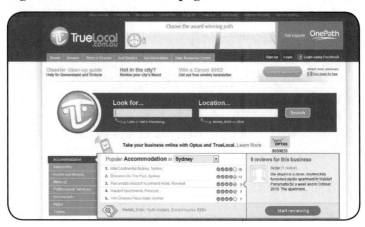

Follow the same principles that applied to filling in the Google form for completing the True Local listing (see figure 2.9). Make sure all your details are correct and ensure you're using keywords relevant to your customers. Fill in as many boxes as you can and make sure opening hours, special offers and popular brands are listed.

Figure 2.9: True Local listing page

True Local also has a coupons feature, so follow the same procedure described for Google Places to add offers, discounts and specials to your entry, which will help it get better results when people search for your product.

In some ways True Local is better for businesses than Google Places, as it allows attachments to be uploaded, which is great for menus, price lists, brochures and other documents. Put up anything that might be useful and name it carefully so the search engines know what it is.

Microsoft Bing

Unbelievably, Microsoft's Bing Local platform works only in the United States and currently has no service in Australia, or any other country, which seriously irritates the Canadians. This failure to execute basically locks them out of the local market, although there are rumours that a local service will be launched any time. Right now, Bing's rather poor local search results are pulled straight from Sensis's Yellow Pages directory.

Sensis

The traditional advertising medium for most Australian small businesses has been the Yellow Pages. If you register with Sensis you will receive a free listing, which will get you in their maps and directories including Microsoft's Bing service.

Sensis's service is fairly limited and it doesn't offer many of the features of True Local or Google Places in its free editions, though the reach of Sensis and the benefit of being in both the print and online Yellow Pages directories mean these listings can be very useful for many businesses.

If you are prepared to pay several hundred dollars a year you can have a web page and email addresses added to your Yellow Pages listing; however, it runs through Sensis's internal booking system, which means you will have to go through the rigmarole of dealing with a salesperson and approving a physical version rather than doing it yourself.

Yahoo!7

Yahoo!7's local business search is more rudimentary than Google's. The simplest way to get onto Yahoo!7's lists is to use their 'Suggest a page' link on their website or the Yahoo! submission process, which will let you add your page for future listing, but little else.

To get a better quality listing in Yahoo!7, you'll need to sign up with True Local, the News Limited online portal. Most of the details you enter into True Local will appear in your Yahoo! listing.

One important angle with Yahoo!7 is their linkages into some of the newer group buying sites and coupon sites. Other services linked into Yahoo!7 include some GPS manufacturers using the Yahoo! Search results in their systems.

Other directories

There are dozens of other free and paid directories and services where you can list your business, but most of them don't have the traction Google and the other big sites have. Most of these sites are dubious in terms of their value and some are poorly disguised scams. Generally it's a good idea to avoid them unless there's a specific advantage in listing with one or two that cater to specific industries or communities.

Conclusion

The free listings are a great way to start establishing an online presence for your business without the time outlay needed to set up a website. If you do have a website, you should join these services as well to get more publicity for your site.

Another step that will help publicise your business for free is getting involved in social media and taking advantage of these free services (see chapter 3).

Checklist

> Have you registered your websites on the following sites: Google, Yahoo!7, Bing and Sensis?

> Are your contact details correct?

> Have you put good descriptions in all available boxes?

> Do photos and other uploaded files have descriptive names?

> Have you created coupons for your special offers?

> Is the information consistent across your listings?

> Are your listings clear on the areas you cover?

Chapter 3
Social media

Nothing illustrates the difference between old media and new media better than social media. Under the old model — newspapers, radio or television — someone owns the platform and publishes information through it. If the audience wants to respond, members send in a letter or call the talkback phone lines. In social media, the audience does the publishing, then members talk to each other about it.

In many ways social media isn't anything new: it's the internet equivalent of hanging around the mall or gossiping in the tea room, and even using internet services like bulletin boards and newsgroups pre-dates the world wide web.

What the newer social media platforms have changed is how people share information. It's now much easier for people with similar interests, backgrounds or family links to connect with each other from anywhere in the world. By joining these networks you will be able to tap into passionate and motivated communities that might, if you show respect to them and their interests, be interested in your products.

And just as you can establish or enhance your web presence using free online listings, you can extend that presence using the free social media sites.

Talking, not shouting

One of the big differences between the traditional media channels and social media is the way you attract attention. In the older media channels, you had to shout in the hope that your product would be seen. This model suited big businesses that have the deep pockets needed to fund a traditional marketing campaign.

For smaller business, the only way to compete with big business campaigns was to be as loud as possible—big billboards, garish print adverts and irritating late-night TV commercials were typical ways of being seen. But even if you were big, you had to be big, loud and brassy.

The social media channels operate more like a conversation, and using the shouting techniques of the traditional sectors will kill your site stone dead. Instead, communicating in social media is about cultivating online relationships by getting people, not always customers, to becoming supporters of your business. They may choose to support your business because they like you, because they think the product's funky, because their friends like you or your products, or for any other of a million possible reasons. In many ways this suits smaller businesses that operate on local reputations and word of mouth—especially because most of us don't have the funds, or the brash personalities, to run loud, abrasive advertising campaigns on TV or radio.

A word about 'free'

One thing that should be kept in mind about all the social media platforms is that these are privately owned businesses, so they are being run with an eye to making a profit. That profit could come from selling your information or feeding your competitors' adverts onto your site. So understand there are some downsides to 'free' services.

Also remember that, as private services, these sites play by their own rules and often tend to take action, without thinking, against what they see as a breach of their rules. As a consequence, many businesses have found themselves suspended without notice for spurious or even incorrect reasons.

One other major trap with social media sites is they can be monstrous time sinks. It's possible to spend an entire day reading and engaging with people on these services. So consider 'free' as meaning 'no monetary cost', since you can spend an amazing amount of time online.

Despite the downsides, the social media platforms are great for generating online traffic and building a business. The biggest, most vibrant—and often strangest—platform of all is Facebook.

Facebook

With more than 500 million users at the end of 2010, and looking at a potential stock market value of over US$50 billion, Facebook has become an internet force to be reckoned with. The Facebook platform has a number of quirks and features that make it unique on the internet.

At the core of Facebook is your network of friends—not necessarily people you know in real life, but folk you have agreed to become Facebook friends with. Your friends can communicate with you, see information you have chosen to keep private from most of the world and invite you to join their games, groups and causes. Those friends can also post on your wall, which is the first screen you see when you go into your Facebook profile page. The wall keeps you up to date with everything your friends are doing, including what they like.

The 'like' button appears on every page or update on Facebook: if you like something someone has said or done, you click the button and your likes will go onto all your friends' walls.

Facebook does not allow businesses to set up personal profiles. Instead, businesses have to set up a Facebook page, which is free and can be customised to suit your business.

It is important for a business to set up and run a a Facebook page as many customers are more active on this social media platform than they are on any other site on the web. In fact, some businesses don't even bother creating a website at all and just make do with a Facebook page.

Although just running a Facebook page is easy and cost-effective, it is something that's best avoided as some businesses have inadvertently fallen foul of Facebook's terms of service (which can be quite strict!) and found their pages shut down for minor matters without notice. It's also important to remember that you want fans to be your customers and exposed only to what you're offering, not simply fans of Facebook.

Probably the best thing about Facebook for the smaller business is that it's a great channel for announcing events and products. However, the service also has the benefits of building up a base of friends and customers. Using it to track customer complaints and the performance of products shouldn't be discounted either, as unhappy clients will post messages to your wall.

To set up a Facebook page go to <www.facebook.com/pages> and click the 'Create page' button in the top left-hand corner. This will take you to the *Create a Page* screen, which gives you the choice of the type of page you prefer.

For most business owners, the choice is between 'Local business' or 'Place of interest' and 'Company, organisation or institution' although 'Product or brand' can be appropriate if you are launching an individual product.

You're not restricted to choosing only one type; you can set up a local business page now and launch individual products or even causes later, so don't worry too much about locking the business into one category or another.

Unfortunately when you create the page you won't be able to choose a username such as www.facebook.com/mybusiness as you need 25 fans before Facebook will allow you to claim the name. You will have to wait until enough people have liked your business before you are able to choose a customer friendly name.

Many businesses overcome this by getting staff, friends and family to like the page straight away, so ask your relatives and social circle to do this as soon as you've registered.

When you choose one of the page options, a sub-screen will appear asking for your basic details, such as location and phone number. Once those questions are answered, you will have your basic Facebook page set up.

From there, you can upload your logo and any other pictures, videos and links to your or other people's interesting websites in a similar way to that described for local business directories (see chapter 2). Try to keep your information consistent across the different platforms.

Even if you don't take social media or Facebook seriously, it's worthwhile checking the page at least every week, just to see what people are saying. If you have something useful to add, such as a special offer or a new product, make sure it goes onto the page.

You can customise your pages with backgrounds and landing pages, which can be complex to set up but effective. More detailed Facebook stategies are discussed later (see step 6), but a basic Facebook page with regular updates is usually enough to get many businesses started.

Mixing personal and business

A common trap for social media users is to mix their personal and professional lives online. This presents a number of risks for the business owner.

The biggest risk is your business becomes too wrapped up in your own persona. For most businesses, this is best avoided as it reduces the sale value of the enterprise when you want to move on.

More dangerously, silly Facebook posts or tweets can get you into trouble. Standards and laws of the offline world apply equally online. What might seem like a harmless joke to you might not be construed as such by others and that can open your business up to bad publicity, or even prosecution under harassment, libel or other laws.

Probably the riskiest thing of all is using social media when you're angry, upset or drunk. If a customer or supplier has raised your blood pressure it's a good idea to go for a walk and avoid using Twitter or Facebook until you have calmed down.

If you are going to use social media in both your personal and business capacities, it's best to set up separate accounts and not mix the two. While Facebook and LinkedIn force you to do this, other sites, including Twitter, Flickr and YouTube, don't. Keep in mind that anything you post in a private or business capacity is available for the world to see.

LinkedIn

Whereas Facebook is the general community site, LinkedIn is more focused on business and recruitment. At its most basic, LinkedIn is like an online CV, where people post their work experience and make connections with people they have worked and dealt with.

LinkedIn also allows you to set up a company page (see figure 3.1), and that's worthwhile, particularly if you stage business-oriented events or if you're recruiting. A company page gives current and previous employees, suppliers or contractors the opportunity to link to your business and follow your news.

Figure 3.1: LinkedIn company page

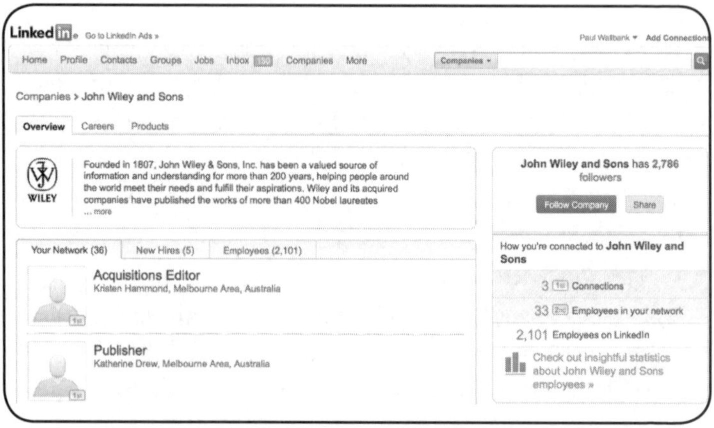

Like Facebook, setting up a LinkedIn company page is a straightforward process of filling in key details about your business. As LinkedIn is checked by Google it's a good opportunity to improve the business's search engine visibility. Typing in similar details to those you entered for Google Local and True Local in the previous chapter is the best way to use LinkedIn well.

If your business mainly deals with other big commercial organisations, government departments or professional groups, then you will find LinkedIn is a particularly powerful tool. Having a comprehensive, up-to-date profile is an indicator to big clients that you are serious in the online space.

Flickr

The main purpose of Flickr is photo sharing. Over time it has also become a powerful social media platform as like-minded people gather online to share photos and interests. Photos posted on Flickr often aren't directly related to the business, but one landscape gardener actually gets business from his wildlife photos. It's more typical that a reception hall might have photos of weddings, and an entertainer will have photos of their performances.

Naturally photographers and artists use the photo-sharing sites to display their portfolios. There's nothing to stop you posting pictures of work you're proud of as a concreter, hairdresser or caterer—just remember to get permission from your client if they can be identified from a photo.

Flickr, and the other photo-sharing sites, can be a very good way to build a community and fan base around your organisation. If you like taking photos, your hobby can become a useful part of your business.

For business, it's straightforward to set up a Flickr profile by visiting <www.flickr.com>, setting up a new account and then posting photos relating to your business. With a link to your website in the profile page, you're creating an online profile that is going to attract the interest of the search engines while spreading the word about your business.

YouTube

Another surprising social media platform is YouTube, the video-sharing service. Many businesses are shooting videos to post on YouTube to promote their products.

As with other social media channels, loud advertisements for the business don't work on this platform, while instructional and informational videos do well while also promoting the business.

A great example of this is Jim the Realtor, a San Diego–based real estate agent who has become famous for taking videos of his inspections and travels around southern California and uploading them on YouTube (see figure 3.2). As well as being entertaining, he gives many good hints on what to watch for, such as badly constructed homes, overhanging powerlines and various vendor tricks.

Often successful businesses on YouTube, like Jim's, don't spend a lot of money on production—though if you have the budget, skills and equipment to do a high-quality video it won't hurt. However, the experience seems to be that online viewers aren't fussed about picture quality when watching videos on a computer or smart phone.

Figure 3.2: Jim the Realtor's YouTube channel

Twitter

Probably the most hyped social media tool through 2009 and 2010, Twitter has become the darling of the media industry, with marketers, public relations firms and journalists flocking to the service. Twitter allows people to send messages from their computers or mobile phones that are no longer than 140 characters, forcing senders, known as tweeps, or twits, to be witty and concise.

Twitter's attractions are that it's a good way to tune into what people you find interesting think, and share their thoughts, ideas and news. As a communication tool, Twitter is as much about listening as talking, so it's a great news delivery tool.

For businesses, Twitter can be an awkward tool to use, as it's probably the biggest time sink on the internet. If you do find really interesting people to follow, you can easily find yourself immersed for the entire day reading fascinating but (distracting) websites.

For startup businesses, it's usually best to sign up to Twitter as a marketing tool, then check in regularly to check what customers are saying about you and what important people are saying about your industry. As you begin to understand how Twitter works and what your circles are like, you can start posting product announcements, communicating with customers and contributing to the conversations you find interesting.

Setting up a Twitter account is quick and easy. Click on the yellow 'Signup' button at the top of the Twitter web page at <www.twitter.com> to set the page up; choose a username — preferably your business name or something very close to it; and put in your email address.

Once you have set up a page in Twitter, you can choose to customise the look and feel of your page using the same techniques described for the other social media platforms (see chapter 2). You can also set up your website to automatically feed new information into Twitter as it's posted.

Conclusion

Social media tools are a good way of getting online for free, as well as being an adequate substitute for smaller or cash-strapped businesses that don't want their own website — although I recommend that every business spends a bit of time setting up a site.

To have a successful presence in social media requires having something useful to say, so you need to have the platform to say something, and that's a basic website, which can be created using free website blogging tools (see chapter 4).

Checklist

> Have you chosen a username close to your business name?

> Have you included unique pictures and videos in your profile?

> Have you linked your social media sites to your other web presences, particularly if you have a website?

> Remember to use social media to listen to your fans and your critics as social media provides a valuable listening post.

> Take care not to be sucked into spending too much time online.

> Try to avoid mixing personal and business in your online presence.

> Don't use social media when you're angry, upset or drunk.

Chapter 4
Blogging platforms

When the web first came along, website development was an expensive process. Many 20-year-olds who had a basic understanding of HTML—the language that web pages are written in—became very rich, and those costs were passed onto the businesses that hired them. As the web has matured, most of the tools to get a website up and running have become easy to use and cheap, or in many cases free, as you will see in this chapter.

Blogs, or web logs, were an early part of the world wide web as the internet gave people an opportunity to create online diaries. Being able to post a regular diary required tools that made it easy to publish online, hence the rise of blogging software. Over time blogging tools have evolved into serious web publishing platforms, and a huge proportion of sites use blogging software to update their content.

Having somewhere to save those sites is also an ongoing problem. Early in the internet years, most free services that offered people a website plastered the pages with advertisements, many of which were ugly and detracted from the brand, look and feel of your site (and your business). These services found the advertising didn't pay their bills, so the reliability of the sites suffered and eventually most of the free website companies folded or slowly withered away after being bought out by big business. They were replaced by the free blogging platforms that were originally intended to act as personal diaries, but which have now evolved into powerful platforms for business sites.

Of the remaining free options, the three main free services are Google's Blogger, the popular Wordpress and Weebly. But there is also the option of using your own internet provider to host your website, although that is often limited to home users.

The downside with the free services is that, with the exception of Google's Blogger, you don't get your own domain name—your own address on the internet (this is further explained in step 2)—with the basic setup, and that can detract from your branding and reduces your flexibility. You will also find that the free sites still put advertisements on your pages, so there's a good chance you will find a competitor's advertisement on your site.

Your internet provider

When you connect to the internet, you use an internet service provider (ISP) that handles all the complex and messy stuff involved in connecting to the world. As well as providing the connection to the Net and an email address, many ISPs also offer a basic web service.

An internet provider's space will have a format along the lines of www.yourprovider.com/~your_account_name, which isn't the most professional look, especially if you put your web address on letterheads, marketing material and business cards—it just doesn't look like you own the site and you haven't been prepared to spend the $100 to register a name of your own.

If you're running the business from home and your internet account isn't a business service, you may also find the provider's terms of service prohibit your using the free website included with a home service for anything but personal use.

Overall, using your internet provider's free space isn't a good move, as it generally looks awful, marks you as a small business that can't afford to spend $100 on a domain name and locks you into that company's service, because you will lose the address if you change providers.

The best alternative is to lease space with a web host (see step 3 for more information); however, hosting involves costs, and free alternatives are available to test ideas out or to get your business up and running in the early days, when cash can be a problem.

Blogger

The oldest and most popular of the blogging platforms is Blogger, which is part of the Google empire. When you sign up with Blogger, you will get a website name along the lines of yourbusiness.blogspot.com, which looks far more professional than the usually clumsy free ISP web addresses.

Having your business name at the front of the address has advantages when potential customers are searching on the

Net, as this style is easier for the search engines to pick up. While it isn't quite as good as having your own domain name, it's a much better look than the internet provider option.

Set up a Blogger site by visiting the Blogger website at <www.blogger.com> and following the free signup process, demonstrated in figure 4.1.

Figure 4.1: set up a new Blogger page

As you can see in figure 4.2, overleaf, you will be asked to verify the name you want to use for site. This is often a problem as many of the good business names have already been taken. You may have to be creative to find a name for your blog that reflects your business name (some ways of getting around a preferred name already being used are discussed in step 2).

Figure 4.2: the Blogger welcome page

Once you have named the page, you will then be prompted to choose a template (see figure 4.3), which sets the layout of the pages of your blog, from a variety on offer. Templates are straightforward and you can change or modify them later. So choose the one you most like the look of, and move on.

Figure 4.3: choose a Blogger template

That's it! You have now finished the basic setup. Click 'Next' and you're taken to your first blog post (see figure 4.4). This is the best place for explaining who you are and what your business does.

Figure 4.4: Blogger post page

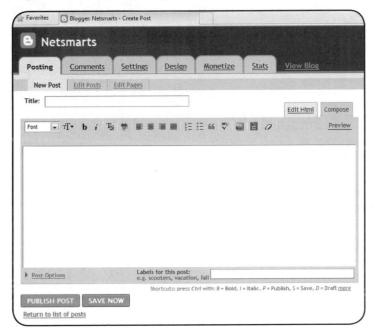

Blogger's great advantage is that it works immediately. Most of the features are built in and, by clicking on the tabs across the top, you can select the key features you want on your page.

The screenshot in figure 4.5, overleaf, shows the layout screen where you can move elements around. You can also use the 'Add gadget' option. By the beginning of 2011, nearly 1200 gadgets were available, doing things like showing lists of the latest posts and inserting maps into your page or displaying advertisements on your site.

Figure 4.5: Blogger design page

Blogger is by far the easiest of all the blog tools for changing your design. For a startup business, particularly one with little spare cash, this is the easiest and quickest way to get online.

It is possible to customise Blogger so it no longer looks like a standard template, but that is harder work than it is on the other platforms. While Blogger isn't really designed for unique layouts, for most businesses it offers a great starting point.

Blogger's great advantage is that Google allows you to use your own domain name for free, making Blogger the best publishing platform for a cost-sensitive startup business. To use your own domain name, click on 'Settings' in Blogger's control panel, select 'Publishing' then click the 'Custom domain' link. Blogger will then take you to the screen where you can enter your domain name or buy a new one through Google's service, which costs $10 a year. (Buying a domain name is discussed in detail in step 2.)

Wordpress

The most popular blogging software is Wordpress, which is steadily becoming the leading web publishing platform. It has a well-developed, if basic, content management system and its vast range of templates can be customised to suit your needs and gives sites a professional look.

Most organisations running Wordpress have the software running on their own servers or on a hosting service (see step 3). However, Wordpress itself offers a basic free service, along with options such as your own domain name and getting rid of the advertisements for a monthly or annual fee.

Like Blogger, the free sites have the format www. yourbusiness.wordpress.com, which is fine, but it gives away the fact your business uses a free service. Wordpress makes some money from offering a premium service that allows you to use your own domain name (see step 3).

To set up a free Wordpress account, the first step is to key the address <www.wordpress.com> into your web browser, where you will find the screen shown in figure 4.6, overleaf. Wordpress is proud of the many sites that use its software. This page can be quite addictive if you like exploring the interesting and quirky parts of the web.

Once you have finished exploring, click on the 'Sign up now' button. Just below the button you will see a 10-step guide to setting up a Wordpress blog. This is worth reading for general information about blogging, even if you aren't planning to use Wordpress.

Figure 4.6: welcome to Wordpress

When you are on the Wordpress *Sign Up* page (see figure 4.7), you will be asked to name your blog, and choose a username, password and contact email address. As on Blogger, you may find your desired name has been taken, so you may have to get creative in choosing a title (see step 2).

Once you have chosen a name, a confirmation will be sent to your email address. Follow the instructions in the email so that Wordpress will know that you are who you claim to be, and you will be able to log on to your Wordpress site.

Figure 4.7: setting up a free Wordpress account

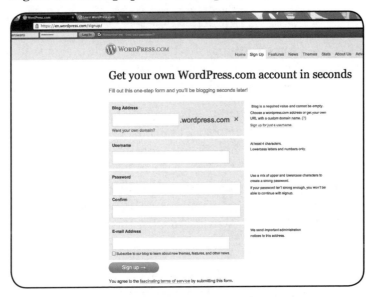

As figure 4.8 shows, the Wordpress site is a much more complex beast than Blogger, so it's worth watching the two-minute *Introduction to the Wordpress dashboard* video so you can find your way around.

Figure 4.8: the Wordpress control panel

The important initial parts of setting up the site are getting the layouts correct and making sure you set the time zone to local settings so people aren't confused by your dates. All of Wordpress's settings are under the 'Settings' tab, and it's best to read through them to ensure all of your business information is entered and correct before posting.

One of the most powerful aspects of Wordpress is the huge range of themes, or templates, available for you to customise your website — in the free version, more than 100 are currently on offer (see figure 4.9). To install any of them it's a simple process of going to the 'Appearance' menu selecting 'Themes', browsing what's on offer, then clicking on whichever one you like and clicking on 'Activate' for that theme to be the new look of your site.

Figure 4.9: Wordpress themes screen

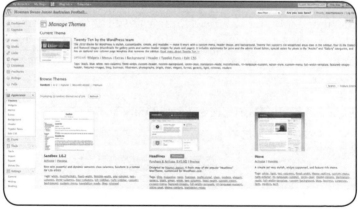

Like Blogger, Wordpress has a whole nest of plug-ins, called widgets. While the free, hosted version of Wordpress offers a limited number of widgets, you can still activate and drop in the built-in ones from the 'Widgets' menu under 'Appearance'.

With the basics set up, it's now time to post your first blog. To send your first post, click the 'Posts' menu and then the 'Add new post' button. The *post* screen, where you can fill in your details and write your first post, is shown in figure 4.10.

Figure 4.10: Wordpress post screen

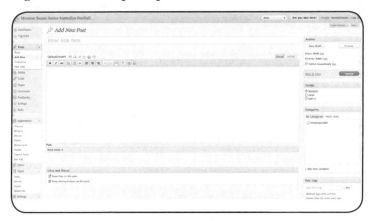

Overall, Wordpress is the best choice for creating an online presence using a blog because it has the easiest upgrade path. If your business is successful, you can scale up a Wordpress site and move it to a more flexible footing as it grows (see steps 3 and 4).

Weebly

The last of the common free platforms is Weebly. Like Blogger, Weebly has a very easy-to-use drag and drop interface, which makes it popular with small businesses.

Weebly gets down to business more quickly than Blogger or Wordpress, and after signing up with a username, password and email, you will find the *Configure a domain* screen illustrated in figure 4.11, overleaf, which shows the options available. If you want to buy a domain name, Weebly will do it for you, but the price is about three times Blogger's charge.

Figure 4.11: Weebly configure a domain screen

One advantage for Weebly is that, because it is not as popular a service as Wordpress or Blogger, it's more likely that your business name will be available there. If you find yourbusinessname.blogger.com is taken on one of the other sites, try the Weebly alternative, which is preferable in search engine terms.

Once you have set up with Weebly (see figure 4.12), it is extremely easy to design and publish pages with a drag and drop screen that lets you change layouts, basic content and even, if you're daring, custom HTML, which requires some knowledge of the basic language of website design.

Figure 4.12: Weebly setup page

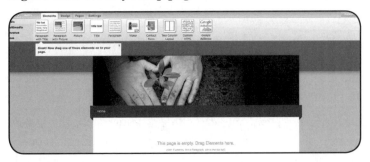

Weebly doesn't offer a great range of plug-ins and templates like Blogger and Wordpress, but it does have an advantage in that the basic needs of a site, such as search engine optimisation (SEO), are built into the free version.

Another of Weebly's built-in functions is an e-commerce feature, which is ready to go for PayPal and Google Checkout (see step 4). This provides an incredibly easy-to-use function for a basic e-commerce setup, but many customers may be reluctant to buy products from an online merchant using a free website.

Like Wordpress, Weebly does have a number of paid add-ons in their Pro version, which costs $67 a year. Pro adds a number of features that improve the custom look of the website.

Weebly's ease of use makes it a good choice for beginners, but it does lack the flexibility of the other platforms. Backing up and copying to other sites can be difficult as well. For a small business that has no intentions of growing, Weebly might meet your needs, but it's difficult to recommend it for bigger businesses.

Other choices

A number of other options for free sites exist, but most of them are more suited to personal blogs, which may work for independent consultants, but probably won't cut it for most businesses.

If you are interested in using one of these sites, the popular three are Tumblr, Amplify and Posterous. They are all adequate blogging platforms, but they lack the level of service and template range of the other three services.

Of the free website choices, Blogger is probably the easiest to use of the platforms, while Wordpress offers a better expansion path for a growing business. Both are great tools and easy to use for posting information.

Conclusion

Adding your information to online listings, using social media and blogging are all ways of creating an online presence for your business—all for no cost, other than the short time it takes to fill in the forms. Your business will start appearing in the results of searches by your customers and prospective customers, while you start working on a website. The first steps in creating your own website are discussed in step 3.

Checklist

> Have you chosen a service that will meet the needs of your business for the next two years? If you're looking at rapid growth, Wordpress is the best.

> Have you secured the same name as your business for your website? If not, have you chosen something close and descriptive?

> Have you investigated the different templates or themes available and chosen one that suits your business?

➤ Are your blog posts at least 500 words?

➤ Have you made sure that the blog post title concisely describes the post's content?

➤ Are you keeping paragraphs short? The web loves white space.

➤ Are you using images to break up the text?

Step 2

The name

Chapter 5

What's in a name?

Step 1 showed you how to create a web presence quickly and easily using some of the free services available on the Net. You will revisit some of these ideas when we talk about the technology available to you in step 3. Now in step 2 we are going to talk about how having your own website, clearly identified with your business name, shows you are serious about your business and how the world sees it.

The importance of a name

Our own name is a fundamental part of our personalities, and that's true of our business as well. In the crowded world that is the internet, we need to give a lot of thought to what our business is, what it does and the name that gives it a unique identity.

One of the worst things you can do is to choose a name that conflicts with that of a larger business or competitor. Resolving a trade name issue is a complex, stressful and always expensive exercise. There is also no guarantee that you will win a dispute, even if you believe there's right on your side.

The founders of Absolut Swimwear found this when they were pulled into a long fight with the makers of Absolut Vodka. The ensuing legal dispute cost them many thousands of dollars and hours of management time. Eventually they had to surrender, because they simply couldn't afford to continue.

Often a business learns they are in a conflict only after they have been operating for a while, so it's embarrassing for the owners and confusing for the customers. By the time you're forced to change your name many key clients and suppliers have the original business title in their address books, accounting programs and everywhere else. A forced name change usually means losing customers, as people think you have gone out of business when the old name disappears.

It's tempting just to use someone else's name and ride on their coat-tails, although this runs the risk that you may end up giving business to a competitor. Given that people are looking for you on the internet, using a competitor's name is a recipe for confusion. My own business, PC Rescue, had this happen when another business registered the name PC Resq. The result was that we found the two businesses being constantly confused. Different customers called us; landlords chased us for our competitor's rent; and different organisations kept contacting us as they mistook us for them. Eventually the other business gave up and moved on, but not before the name had caused problems for both of us.

So how do we ensure we have a safe, unique name for our business that is going to get us found online, make sense to our customers and not get us into legal hot water?

Google search

The most obvious first step in choosing a name is to get out and search. Check out your business name with inverted commas around it. Search for 'joe's doughnut shop' then check alternative spellings, names without apostrophes and any other variation that you think might work.

Just because there is a 'Joey's Donut Shop' in rural Wisconsin doesn't mean you can't use the name, but be aware that if your business plans involve setting up branches in the US Midwest, then you'll need to factor that into your plans. A good example of this was when the US chain Burger King opened in Australia. The US company had years before sold the Australian naming rights to a local businessman, who had also registered the Burger King trademarks. The US company found they couldn't operate in Australia under their own name. Worse, the similar branding confused the market. Eventually Burger King gave up and now Aussies know the chain as Hungry Jack's—Jack surprisingly being the name of the local businessman they spent years fighting.

So the first step is to make sure no-one else is selling under the name you want, whether that means they are big enough to monster you or that your customers and suppliers are going to be confused.

Oh no, my name is taken!

While the internet is a big place, so too is the human imagination, and the sad truth is the fantastic name you have thought of may already have been taken.

You will usually find on the first page of a Google search if that's the case and then it's time to be creative.

It may be that it doesn't matter. If the name of your patisserie in Ballarat is the same as that of a landscape gardener in Wisconsin, then you can probably use it without any problems, particularly if you don't intend ever to trade in Wisconsin.

You may also be able to use it if there's already a similar business in your area, if you can show there is no risk of confusion. Before doing that, you should get professional legal advice and forget it if the name is being used by a large company.

If that's the case, or the lawyer says 'no', then you will have to get creative. Open your computer's word processer, type in the name and use the synonym function on the parts of the name. You may find a better name from just mixing and matching different words.

Altering the name, for instance so that 'rescue' becomes 'resq' or 'easy' becomes 'EZ' can work, but you may still face problems if another business owner claims a similar title.

If your name is for use on a certain platform, like the free Blogger or Weebly site, you can look at using a different tool or making the name a plural.

Sometimes it is frustrating finding a name that hasn't been used, but it makes good sense to get a unique, defendable name for branding, for legal reasons and for when you want to sell your business.

Domain search

The next step is to search the domains available. To do this, go to the bigger and more popular domain registrars, the organisations that keep track of who owns which domain.

The bigger registers cover a number of different countries and types, so you'll get an idea of just how popular or difficult to get the name is.

There is also a number of different types of domain to consider (see chapter 7). The important ones are the dot. com (.com) and the ones for the specific countries you intend to operate in.

A typical search for a domain is shown in figure 5.1. In this case the registrar offers a range of countries and domain types.

Figure 5.1: domain search results

Remember, your domain name needs to be consistent with your brand or brands. If you intend to move into a new market in the future and the domain name is taken, you may have to buy it later, which can be expensive, but it is an option if all obvious alternatives are taken.

Social Media Search

Social media tools like Twitter, Facebook and MySpace may be important to your business (see step 1). You can visit each site you think you will need, but tools such as the Social Media Search site will check all of them for you (see the *eBusiness* website at <www.ebusinessbook.com.au>).

While you may not use social media tools immediately, it's a good idea to see what is available for your business, and register those names as soon as you can. Good names tend to be snapped up and the social media sites also tend not to shut down names that haven't been updated for some time.

Business name search

The biggest issue is whether your name is already in use by a competitor or someone who could be confused with you. So it's important to check your name is safe and won't cause legal problems down the track.

In some countries, such as Australia, New Zealand and the United Kingdom, there are centralised databases of all business names. For the United States and Canada, each state or province has its own registration process and there's no central database; the same is true for Europe.

Just because a name doesn't appear in the search engines or in the domain registration pages, it doesn't mean that name isn't being used. Some organisations haven't developed their online presence at all, which is one of the reasons this book was written.

You will need to do a business name search in the relevant state, federal and international jurisdictions to ensure your name hasn't been taken. Keep in mind that, in Australia, you can register a business name in one state even if it has been registered in another state. However, you may still hit legal problems if there's a risk of confusion or trademarks have been registered.

Trademark search

Trademarks are possibly the most dangerous area for any business, and intellectual property law is a complex area, meaning lawyers in the field are insanely expensive. So it's best not to fall foul of trademark law if you can avoid it.

While you can register your business names, products and logos as trademarks — and you should do so in every country where you intend to trade — keep in mind that this still does not totally protect you should you come up against a well-funded, determined competitor. However, registered trademarks are good enough to scare off smaller copycats.

Given you don't want to be a smaller copycat, you will need to do a search. The first step is to search on the IP (intellectual property) Australia ATMOSS database (see figure 5.2, overleaf), followed by searches of the US Patents and Trademark Office and any other markets you intend to trade in. Most countries and the European Union do have centralised databases for checking trademark information.

If you are considering trading overseas, the services of a good patent attorney are indispensable. While they can cost a lot, they can help you avoid lengthy and expensive disputes down the track.

Figure 5.2: Australian ATMOSS database search

Always remember that intellectual property law is skewed against the little guy and is very complex. If you feel uneasy about the results you find in a trademark search, then it's best to pick another name.

Language issues

An area to be very careful with is the translation of your business name. What could be a really clever name in your own language could be hilarious or embarrassing in someone else's native tongue. It's not just different languages that might give you trouble, either: words can mean different things in different forms of the same language. Consider the US meaning of the expression 'to root for', which has a very different meaning in Australia.

These regional and dialect differences can't be overstated in bigger markets. If you're intending to sell into southern China, for instance, checking the meanings of words in Cantonese as well as Mandarin is a good idea. Similarly getting a Canadian Quebeçois to check the wording of a product you're launching into France or French-speaking Africa could have humiliating results, as there are so many regional differences in the language.

International concerns

Regardless of whether a country speaks your language or not, you need to have local advice to overcome the quirks of the target market. You may find that licences are required to operate a business; special labelling rules apply; or you need to be aware of other cultural and legal aspects.

Even if you don't want to engage a local partner or agent, it's probably worthwhile speaking to trade organisations or other businesses working in those countries. Many bigger cities have chambers of commerce representing those who trade with particular countries.

Other intellectual property concerns

Keep in mind some other intellectual property areas can trap you with a business name, such as copyright and 'passing off'. These are complex matters that you will need a lawyer to deal with if you suspect they are areas you might become involved in.

Generally, however, most intellectual property naming disputes revolve around names that are in business use, so spending a few minutes on an internet search usually picks up any problems with a proposed name.

Names are important to your business: it is a valuable asset and, hopefully, when you grow the business, you will want to sell all or part of it. What's more, every business is unique—just like a person—and its name is a crucial part of the organisation's identity. So spending some time ensuring the name isn't going to be easily confused or attract the wrath of a big corporation's lawyer is critical to getting online and being seen among the millions of different internet names.

Conclusion

Having established that you can use your preferred business name, or having found a good alternative, you need to think about the domain name, such as .com.au, to use for your business. Some types of domain have particular qualifications you have to meet to get the domain name you want, and the name needs to be close to your business and what your customers expect. The next chapter takes you through all the possibilities.

Checklist

➤ Does your business name already appear in Google searches?

➤ Are the domain names you want available?

➤ Is your business name being used in the markets you intend to operate in?

➤ Has your business name been registered in your home market?

➤ Are there any trademarks associated with your business name?

➤ Is the name recognisable and does it make sense to your customers?

➤ Are your business names consistent across platforms?

Chapter 6

Types of domain

Once you have established the business name, you need to register the domain name—a domain name can be thought of as being your street address on the internet, such as microsoft.com or pcrescue.com.au, or the bit that comes after the 'www.' in a web address. If you don't register one, you're forced to use others' services rather than owning your own internet property.

Registering domain names is probably the most complex and frustrating aspect of getting a business onto the internet. Aside from the obvious choice of the .com.au domain name, there's a whole range of domain names to confuse the issue.

This chapter is by far the most technical and jargon laden in the book, so if you don't want to be swamped with technical details, get a .com.au domain for your business and be done with it. However, an Australian commercial name is not right, or even available, for everyone.

What is a domain?

Simply put, a domain is the human-friendly part of an internet address. Rather than dealing with machine-oriented numbers like 207.46.232.182 or 61.8.0.59 that computers use to find a website, people can type in easier to remember domain names such as for <www.ebusinessbook.com.au> or <www.amazon.com>.

While this is simple in principle, there's a lot of terminology involved. A domain name itself is made up of two parts: the top level domain (TLD), which is the .com, .org, .com.au, or .nz.gov part of the name; and the name itself, which is the organisation's part. Put the two together and we have the universal resource locator, known as the URL.

Choosing the domain name

Sometimes a search shows that the obvious domain names are already taken and you have to investigate alternatives, such as .net.au domains. Some organisations are better served by .asn.au or .edu.au names which are designed for associations and educational institutions. If you intend to sell overseas, you will also have to consider the domains available in the markets you sell into. So for instance a .ca domain is helpful if you're selling to Canadian customers, while a .cn domain is important for the mainland Chinese market.

Choosing the right type of domain is important, as a descriptive domain name helps search engines rank your site. Web-surfers also make assumptions about addresses—automatically assuming your site finishes in .com.au or .com—and many web browsers have an auto-fill feature, which attempts to guess what the user wants as they type it in. Overall it's best to keep your domain name close to your business name.

To make things even more complex, internet search engines have a habit of making guesses based on the searcher's location, so a search for a particular name will return Australian addresses first if your computer appears to be in Australia.

Confusion reigns in the Bigpond

Telstra's consumer internet service, Bigpond, originally gave its customers bigpond.com email addresses, which caused confusion for many Australian internet users who added the .au to the end out of habit.

Later, with the introduction of broadband internet, Telstra decided to give its subscribers on the faster cable and ADSL connections a bigpond.net.au address, which further confused their customers and anyone who sent an email to one of their users.

Eventually Bigpond settled on the bigpond.com.au address, but, even today, 13 years later, Bigpond addresses still confuse people.

If you do own several domains—which is a good idea for most businesses—it is fairly easy to point them to the same internet location so they all lead to the one address and ensure your customers don't get confused.

Explaining the DNS

Once a new domain name is approved it goes into a massive list called the Domain Name Service (DNS), which translates the internet protocol (IP) addresses used by computers into straightforward, familiar names like google.com, whitehouse.gov, abc.net.au, and pcrescue.com.au. The basic function of an internet service provider (ISP) is to make sure its customers are connected to the DNS servers so that people can find websites. The DNS is an essential part of the internet's workings.

The domain name is more than a web address though. It can provide any service the owner of a computer connected to the internet wants, or wants to offer, such as email, file transfers, file sharing or any of hundreds of other things you can do on the Net. The prefix or protocol—the letters placed at the front of website addresses—indicates to other computers what is in the data: http is used for web pages but there are many other protocols in use, as explained in table 6.1.

Table 6.1: typical internet protocols

Abbreviation	Meaning	Uses
http	Hypertext transport protocol	Websites
https	Hypertext transport protocol secure	Secure websites
mms	Microsoft streaming	Media files
ftp	File transport protocol	Copy files across the Net
pop	Post office protocol	Collects emails
smtp	Simple mail transfer protocol	Sends emails
smb	Simple message block	Windows networks
skype	n/a	Skype networking

The types of domain

Different top level domains indicate the nature of your organisation, as shown in table 6.2. A government organisation has .gov as its domain. An Australian government organisation has .gov.au, while a branch of the New South Wales state government has .nsw.gov.au.

Table 6.2: common top level domains (TLDs)

Types of domain	Used by
.com	Commercial organisations
.coop	Cooperatives
.edu	Educational establishments
.gov	Government entities
.info	Information sites
.int	International organisations established by treaty
.mil	Military forces
.mobi	Mobile devices
.name	Families and individuals
.net	Originally for internet organisations
.org	Originally for non-commercial organisations

Country-specific domains

The country-specific names define your business as part of that country, so if you are operating in multiple countries it's best to register domains in each nation. So a business operating in New Zealand should make sure it has the relevant .co.nz domain name. See table 6.3 on p. 77 for a selected list of domains.

While US organisations dominate the top level .gov and .com domains, those domain names are actually international. A .us domain actually exists, along with a domain for each US state, although these aren't very popular with government organisations.

The attraction of .com domains is they can be ridiculously cheap and have no rules on eligibility—you can just grab and use them. This ease of registration—in the next chapter we look at how you register them—is also a downside as many of the good names have been taken.

There are some interesting quirks in the country names as different governments have varying rules, the .tv domain belongs to the country of Tuvalu in the South Pacific, but it is run by a company part owned by the Tuvalu government and the US company Verisign, which sells the domains to online television businesses.

A similar quirk exists with the Libyan domain name, .ly, which has been used for address shortening services, such as bit.ly. At present there is some question on the authority of the .ly domain, so it may be that the rules and sites running on it will change in the near future.

Ideally, most businesses will register .com for their worldwide operations and the country-specific codes for their target markets. There's no global rule to say you can't register in multiple countries or domains, although the various national administrators tend to frown on this.

For businesses operating only in Australia, a .com domain on its own can be a problem, as Australian web users tend to automatically include the .au on the end of most addresses. When Telstra rolled out Bigpond with the bigpond.com email addresses, users' tagging .au on the end was a very common reason for emails not being delivered.

If you are operating only in Australia, then the .com.au domain is probably your best bet. Another advantage with the .au domains is that they are much more tightly controlled than most others, which means it's more likely the name you want is available. You can also choose .net.au or .org.au domain names.

Keep in mind, too, that every country has its own domain, so you need to tailor your domains accordingly if you're going to trade with those countries. For instance, if you are selling into New Zealand, South Africa or China, registering the .nz, .za or .cn domain is necessary.

Table 6.3: list of selected country domains

Domain	Country	Domain	Country
.at	Austria	.my	Malaysia
.au	Australia	.nl	Netherlands
.br	Brazil	.nz	New Zealand
.ca	Canada	.pg	Papua New Guinea
.ch	Switzerland	.ru	Russian Federation
.cn	China	.sg	Singapore
.de	Germany	.th	Thailand
.eu	European Union	.tp	East Timor
.fr	France	.tr	Turkey
.gb	Great Britain	.uk	United Kingdom
.hk	Hong Kong	.us	United States
.ie	Ireland	.va	Holy See (Vatican
.il	Israel		City State)
.jp	Japan	.za	South Africa

As you can see can see from the list, not every country's domain name makes sense, and sometimes a nation even gets a bonus domain: for instance, .uk and .gb are both available for British addresses.

Each country appoints its own organisation to administer who does what with their internet domains and so the rules on eligibility for registering vary between nations. Some countries, such as China and Italy, insist only locals can register their domain names, while others, such as the United Kingdom and New Zealand, have very open policies.

In Australia, you should only register a domain name that is closely associated with your business name or products. While it's rare to be caught out, you may find someone else objecting to your use of a similar name. If possible, play within the rules so that you don't end up in a messy dispute.

Alternative domain types

There is also the option of using alternative domains, such as .net and .biz, if the more common domains we discussed earlier are taken (see table 6.4). Because these aren't common you might find your customers get confused, as web-surfers tend to assume addresses are .com or the commercial domain for their country, such as .com.au or .co.nz.

Table 6.4: List of alternative domains

Domain name	Used by
.asia	Companies, organisations and individuals in the Asia–Pacific region
.biz	Businesses
.cat	Catalan language/culture sites
.jobs	Employment-related sites
.museum	Museums

Industry domains

There are some domains for specific industries, but most of these domains are really thinly guised revenue ploys for ICANN, the domain name authority. You might find some of the domain names in table 6.5 useful, but most aren't popular.

Table 6.5: Industry-specific domains

Domain name	Used by
.aero	Air transport industry
.pro	Certain professions, such as lawyers
.tel	Telephone and internet services
.travel	Travel agents, airlines, hoteliers, tourism bureaus, etc.

While these industry-specific domains may be used in your business sector, keep in mind that most customers won't be used to them, so they are probably best for specialist use within those industries rather than for client-facing sites.

Domain traps

If you find a domain name, it's worthwhile checking if a similar business already owns the .com domain. I had this problem with the pcrescue.com.au domain, because pcrescue.com was owned by computer business in the US.

To compound the confusion, there was also a software product called PC Rescue. Googling PC Rescue brought up our business first and our American namesake second, which meant both of us had a regular stream of cranky customer billing and support requests for the software product, which appeared at number eight in the search results.

So it's worthwhile doing a good web search on your name before registering any domain, just to avoid any confusion or the risk of stepping on another enterprise's trademark.

So the .com.au domain is important, as is the .com domain, and registering both should be a high priority for every business. If you find all the domains are available for your business or product, then you should register in every country you intend to operate, in order to protect your name.

Conclusion

Having decided which type of domain names you want to use, the next step is to register them. The next chapter looks at domain registrars—the organisations responsible for registering and controlling who gets a domain name.

Checklist

➤ Do you qualify for all the domains you want?

➤ Are the available names close to your business or product?

➤ Will your customers expect a .com or a .com.au address?

➤ Which countries do you operate in, or plan to operate in?

➤ Is the name available in those countries?

➤ Is the .com or other top level domain (TLD) available?

➤ Are there industry-specific domains relevant to your business?

Chapter 7

Choosing a registrar

Once you have decided on your business name and checked the availability in various domains, it's time to register your domain name. Registering a domain is one of the fiddly things about creating your own a website. The process can be bureaucratic and sometimes irritating, but thankfully it's rarely expensive.

Managing more than 120 million domain registrations is beyond any one organisation. To overcome this, each of the different domain types (described in chapter 6) has its own administrator who in turn appoints registrars to handle the messy work of dealing with site owners.

Before you can set up your website, you have to register the domain with an appropriate registrar. This is usually painless, albeit with sometimes irritating paperwork, and relatively cheap, but it does have a few traps.

What does a registrar do?

The registrar's role is to assign the domain name, the bit that comes after the www or @ symbol. For instance, the domain name of Microsoft is microsoft.com.

Each type of domain—the top level domain, or TLD, including .com, .com.au, .org or any of the dozens of other domain types described in chapter 6—has its own registrar. These registrars are accredited by the Internet Corporation for Assigned Names and Numbers (ICANN), which is responsible for keeping track of the domains on the internet.

Registrars take a fee from the owners of the domain names to maintain the DNS records discussed in the previous chapter. That fee, plus the cost of maintaining the lists and a varying amount of profit, are all passed on as a charge to domain holders.

Country designations

As discussed in chapter 6, each country also has its own top level domain—for Australia it's .au; for New Zealand, .nz; for Canada, .ca; and for the UK, .uk—with individual domain authorities for each.

Each of the national registrars has its own registration rules. China only allows Chinese nationals to register .cn names; others, such as Australia, have strict rules on the eligibility of business names and their registration. Because each country has its own rules, it's important to have local advice when registering a name.

The United States tends to think of the top level domains, such as .com and .gov, as belonging to them, though there's a .us domain available for US-based businesses, but the .us domain hasn't caught on in the way the top level domains have.

Some registrars can provide services for many different countries, while others work with only one nation. There's nothing wrong with using one registrar for multiple locations, but be aware that the cheapest registrar for one country's domain might be the most expensive for another's.

Costs

Registering a domain name is just like registering a car in that it needs to be regularly renewed—thankfully without the compulsory insurance and fat taxes. The cost of registration varies between countries and types of registration, so a .com has different fees and criteria from the .edu, which in turn has different costs from a .com.au, .co.nz or .edu.uk. These costs vary between the different registrars licensed to issue names: for instance, in Australia a domain name can cost from $10 a year to $120 for two years.

Often the registration is free if you sign up for a website hosting package with the registrar or the associated company. This is not a good idea for most businesses, as these deals rarely offer useful features or value for money. The other downside of a hosting package with the registrar is the risk of a dispute disrupting your operations, as that registrar becomes a single and vital point in all your internet communications. For that reason, I recommend keeping the two functions with different companies.

The dangers of bundling

Domain registration is not the most profitable business going. As the internet has developed, more registrars have appeared on the market and prices have plummeted. As a consequence, registrars will do anything they can to make more profit from their customers. An obvious area is web hosting—the actual running of the websites rather than just providing an address—which has the advantage of offering the customer a one-stop shop, relieving the time-poor business owner of another set of paperwork.

Generally these deals aren't great for the domain owner, as they tend to be more expensive than separating hosting from domain registration, and they introduce a single point of failure—if the registrar's systems go down, the registrar goes broke or the registrar is thrown out of the system for shonky behaviour (this happens), then both the hosting and the registration will be affected.

Researching registrars

Finding a registrar is a matter of doing a search on your favourite search engine to find what's on offer. Figure 7.1 shows the Go Daddy registration page, with the domains available and extra features. Once you think you have found the right registrar for you, at the right price, it's easy to check them out by searching on their name.

One trap to watch with registrars is that the domain registration business is very low margin and the real profits lie in web hosting and design, so often there will be offers for cheap or free registrations coupled with hosting and design packages. However, these are rarely good deals. In addition, registrars have been known to engage in unethical behaviour to improve their margins. Some tricks have included selling 10-year registrations, when the maximum available is two, padding out invoices, charging for unwanted add-ins or even giving away your personal details to other companies offering commissions.

Figure 7.1: Go Daddy domain registration

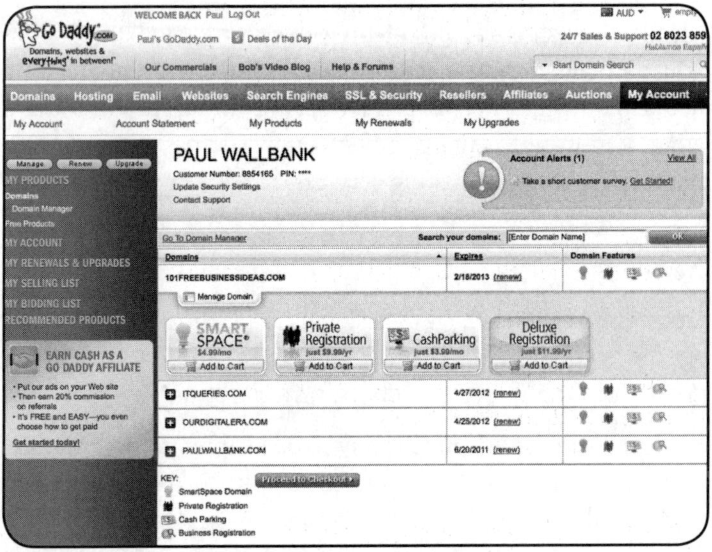

The things to look for in a registrar include reliability, the configuration tools they use, and their service, pricing and billing practices.

Reliability

How reliable is the registrar? Do they have a reputation for prompt service or are they slow? Webmasters live online and are vocal when they encounter these problems. A search through the various webmaster forums, such as Whirlpool <www.whirlpool.net.au>, will quickly locate complaints. If you do find a wave of complaints online, note the dates the comments were made, as some providers pick up their game over time. Sometimes you will find the complaints tail off as the registrar figures out what they are doing.

Configuration tools

Ideally a registrar should offer a web control panel that allows you to make changes to the various business and hosting details yourself. That saves a lot of time and double handling when you want to change any settings, such as your address, authorised users or hosting services.

Service

Does the registrar have a reliable call centre you can call should something go wrong? Call centre and support hours are an important factor in choosing a registrar.

Some registrars don't provide any phone support, doing all their communications by email—which is a fat load of good when your email is down due to their mistake—while many are only 9 to 5 operations. If you choose overseas registrars in a different time zone, then you may find their working hours are different from yours. Factor this in when you are considering pricing.

Pricing

How do the registrars' prices compare? Are they overly expensive or too cheap to be true? The internet is a great place to find fantastic deals that turn out not to be so good.

Generally you will find that most of the domain registrar prices bunch together, with a few outliers who are suspiciously—and unsustainably—cheap or outrageously expensive, and are either trading on ignorance or with cash-happy corporations and government departments.

In 2011, a typical price for a .com.au domain is around $70 for two years, while a .com will cost about $10 a year. Registrars offering names as part of a hosting deal were around $20 for an Australian site.

Billing

Does the registrar offer automated billing and is it very eager to get a payment instruction out of you? Often the indicator of a business that struggles with cash flow is its insistence on having a standing payment order that is difficult to cancel.

Some of the less reputable suppliers also have a habit of charging you early. For instance, if your domain expires in November, they may invoice your renewal in March. While there's nothing illegal about this, it does open you up to risk if the registrar fails or you decide to go elsewhere in the meantime.

Registration details

When you register a domain name, you will have to provide a number of details, including your business address and, for some types of domains, why you qualify for that domain.

For Australian .com.au domains, there is a requirement that the domain has some link with the business. While in the past this was defined extremely narrowly, today the link can be quite tenuous, with the only requirement being that you have a legitimate connection to the name you want to register.

Once you have signed up with the registrar, you will be asked to provide the server settings or redirection. If you don't provide your settings, anyone trying to reach your website will either get a 'not found' message or be sent to a registers holding page, telling the world how you haven't got around to filling in the important details.

If you are hosting your service with the registrar, then they will fill in the details themselves. To follow the recommended path of hosting by someone else, you'll need to provide the name server settings, often called the A Record or CNAME settings, which can be provided by your hosting company (see step 3). Figure 7.2 shows how the Netregistry page allows you to configure an Australian domain.

Figure 7.2: Netregistry domain page

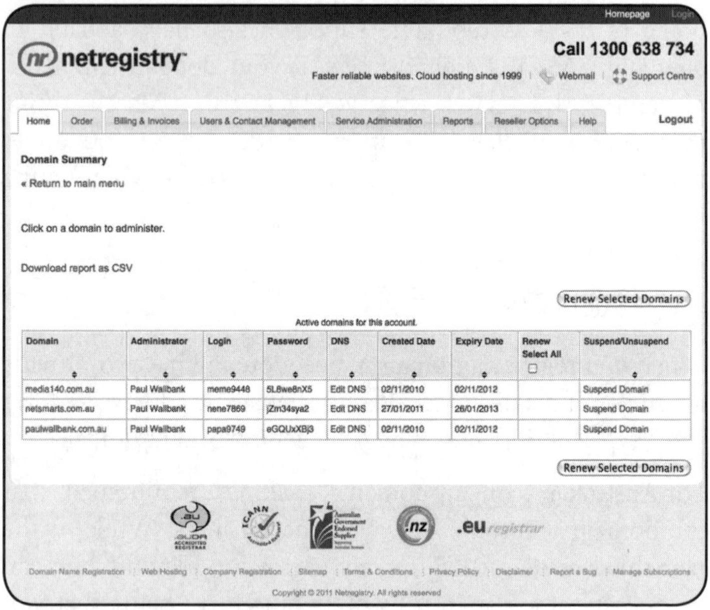

Once all those things are set up, it will take several hours, sometimes up to a day, for the name's registration to take effect. The time varies, as different internet providers update their details with the master DNS servers that control the lists at different times. Normally your hosting company or registrar will advise you that updates will take 24 hours, though you may find changes happen within an hour or two.

One trap with domain names is the administrator addresses. These are the contact details for billing, administration and technical issues. Some registrars try to keep these to themselves in order to control communications from the domain authorities to you, the domain name holder. It's best to ensure your business details are filled in so you receive all correspondence about your important web asset.

Conclusion

In most cases, registering the domain gives you the right to use that domain for a certain period of time. You also need to consider how you are going to use the domain and who will host the domain for you. That might be the registrar or another service provider. We look at hosting in step 3.

Checklist

➤ Are the registrar's prices right?

➤ Does the registrar have an easy-to-use control panel

➤ Is there a hard sell for other services? This is not a good sign.

➤ Does the registrar cover the domain names you want to use?

➤ Are admin, technical and billing names assigned to your company?

➤ Does the registrar's support service have extended, local hours available by phone, email and other means?

➤ Does the registrar have a good reputation?

Step 3

The technology

Chapter 8

Hosting your site

Once you have registered the domain name for your website, your next step is to make the decision about who will host it. Hosting is important, as hosts are the computers that store your website, email and other internet services and look after all the fiddly but essential details of security and reliability. The registrar you have chosen for your domain may offer you a package that includes hosting your site, but that may not be the best choice for you (see step 2). This chapter focuses on how to choose the best host for your website.

While it might look intimidating, the internet is really just a big group of computers talking to each other. Everything online is kept on a computer somewhere, which connects through the Net to all the other computers in the world. For websites, those computers are called web hosts or servers.

Cloud computing

The term cloud computing started appearing around 2008. It relates to the idea of hundreds, and often thousands, of computers working together to offer fast, high-capacity services.

Google and Amazon are the best examples of cloud computing providers, both of them have massive server farms made up of tens of thousands of cheap, easily replaced computers.

No single computer in the massive array is essential to the workings of the system, and if one fails the others pick up the load and continue as if nothing has happened. No data is lost and users don't notice any interruption to their services. This allows services such as Google to run highly reliable, fast applications that would otherwise be beyond the most expensive supercomputers—which isn't to say the server farms themselves are cheap: their electricity bills are so great the farms tend to be built near power stations so they have a convenient source of energy.

Cloud computing is one of the drivers of the internet and why services like web hosting are so cheap. Most web hosting companies and big commercial websites use cloud technologies because they can offer good prices while providing a reliable service. Regardless of the option you choose, it's likely the cloud will be involved somewhere.

Any computer, however old or decrepit, can be a server and if you have the technical knowledge and equipment there's nothing to stop you running an internet host on your own system. In fact, many servers providing the massive cloud computing services are actually cheap computers run in parallel with each other to give the appearance of a super computer. However, running a server exposed to the internet is a complex, full-time job requiring specialist skills, 24-hour support and high quality—read expensive—internet connections, so it's best to leave hosting to a specialist hosting company.

The hosting company basically provides the computers, known as servers, that give the information out to the internet. As part of their service, they will include various things, such as email, data storage, security, software and reporting services that make your online life easier.

Of all the important parts of running a website, the hosting is critical. If your host is unreliable or inadequate, your online presence will be affected. The company you hire to host your website is the equivalent of a landlord, and you need to know that the landlord is reliable and lets your customers onto your site.

Choosing a hosting company

Hosting companies come in all shapes and sizes, from a nerd with some old computers in a spare room, to massive dedicated data centres. In Scandinavia and Britain, enterprising hosting companies offering super secure services have taken over disused missile bunkers and air raid shelters because of their backup power and air conditioning facilities.

Depending upon your needs, you will find hosting companies that do everything for you, right down to designing your website. Others will provide nothing but some blank space on their servers. High-end corporate hosting services don't even provide that, offering instead a locked area with ultra reliable power and internet connections where the client can install their own computers.

Most businesses, though, don't want the hassle and cost of providing their own equipment, so I will assume you will be looking for a provider that does most of the arcane work of keeping servers running and your website online. The only thing you want to hear from your hosting company is the bill—and that should be as small as possible.

A word on SLAs

One term all outsourcing and internet services use when discussing guarantees that their services will work is SLA—or service level agreement—which promises to give you a refund if they fail to meet certain standards.

While these promises sound good, they actually aren't really worth much, as the real problem is disruption to your business. So getting a month's refund on a service outage that has caused havoc for your business and customers is little comfort for the time and stress it has caused you.

SLAs are fine as part of a service provider's guarantees, but you should never assume they are going to cover even a fraction of the costs should you hit a problem. That's why it's important to choose a good provider.

The budget for a hosting company varies according to the services they offer, but you need to keep in mind that cost is not necessarily indicative of quality of service and that many high-priced services offer less than some budget providers. In choosing a hosting company there are a number of factors to consider.

Reputation

The reputation of a hosting company is paramount: an unreliable service will affect your website and reflect badly on your business. You have to make sure your provider is going to be reliable.

A web search is the best and quickest way to find out what the market thinks of your service. It's also worthwhile having a look at some of the online forums. For Australians, the Whirlpool website at <www.whirlpool.net.au> is probably the best (see figure 8.1).

Figure 8.1: Whirlpool web hosting forum

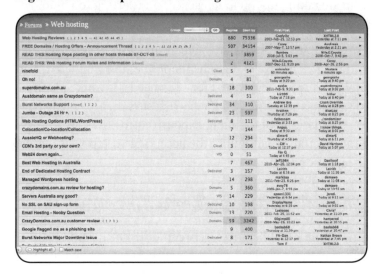

Data allowances

Many hosting services have a fixed data allowance included in their base price. Every time a customer looks at your page, they are downloading some information to their computer. How much they download depends upon what you have on your site. If you have a lot of images or video, then you can expect your site to transfer a lot of data.

Moving data around is a major cost for hosting companies, who are charged hefty commercial rates by the telcos, so they watch their customer's traffic closely and usually have a monthly data allowance for each client. If you exceed the allowance, they then charge a fee per megabyte. Excess data traffic can get expensive, so if a hosting company charges these fees, you should first confirm that you can go up to the next plan without penalty if the traffic is more than you expect.

Some services offer unlimited data plans, but these are subject to acceptable use policies and they often kick out customers who are taking up too much space, transferring too much, or hogging the provider's connection.

For most small businesses, which are just serving websites and have some basic documents online, the unlimited plan providers are probably best for your needs. If you're planning to stream video or have a media-rich site, then you may have to consider one of the more expensive providers, as you will almost certainly fall foul of the acceptable use policies of the cheaper services.

Shared versus dedicated hosting

One of the big differences between different hosting plans is that the cheaper plans offer shared hosting, while the more expensive services provide dedicated hosting. Figure 8.2 shows SmartyHost, a shared hosting provider, and their small business plans.

As the name suggests, dedicated hosting provides a single machine to host your website and internet protocol (IP) address for each account. Naturally that's more expensive than sharing the same computer and IP address around a number of customers.

Shared hosting spreads the cost around a group of customers, sometimes hundreds, so each site has the same IP address and sits on the same big computer. Naturally each customer can't see the others' servers.

Figure 8.2: SmartyHost hosting page

Source: copyright © 2011 MYOB Technology Pty Ltd.

The advantage of shared hosting is that it allows providers to offer very cheap deals. The downside is that if one customer on that shared server has a problem it can affect everyone who shares the space with them.

Dedicated hosting overcomes that problem by providing each customer with their own unique address and space—though naturally that will be much more expensive. Some services offering dedicated hosting don't really offer separate machines, instead using a technology called virtualisation, which allows one computer to pretend it's a number of different systems. Virtualisation is a good midway point between the expensive option of dedicated hosting and cheap as chips shared hosting, but you should be aware that the cheaper dedicated plans are really virtual machines.

In itself virtual machines and shared services aren't a bad thing and they are fine for a business with relatively modest demands. Probably the greatest risk with a shared service is that spam checkers sometimes confuse emails coming from the same server.

Another risk for businesses using the same server is fast growth. If you're in the lucky position that your business goes through a period of rapid expansion you might find the servers can't deal with the traffic. Usually in that situation the hosting company will politely suggest you move up to a dedicated hosting plan.

The higher priced proprietary services like Rackspace tend to deal with the intial stages of growth quite well, as they tend to have well thought out product maps that cater for rapidly expanding businesses. Of course the idea is they will make more money as you grow.

Where problems can arise with these platforms is that it can be difficult to move your site across to a bigger provider or bring it in-house should your business reach the size where the smaller and mid-level solutions just don't cut it. Anyone who was using Twitter in 2008 when it reached several million users will know just how frustrating those growing pains can be for users and businesses.

For most businesses the shared service is the best way to go unless you have specific needs or will be generating the sort of traffic that will overwhelm everyone else sharing your servers.

Control panel

A good hosting company makes it as easy as possible to change settings on your site (see figure 8.3). Ideally it will have an easy to use control panel that will allow you or your webmaster to make basic changes, add new users and update features.

Figure 8.3: bluehost site administration screen

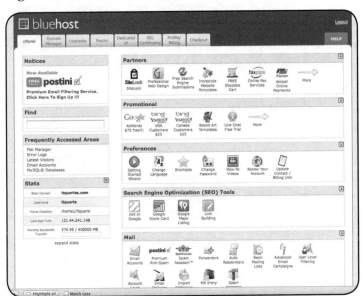

Support services

Ideally you would like to be able to log into your control panel and make changes, but that's not always possible and a call to the support line may be necessary. Before choosing a supplier make sure that they offer support during the hours you operate — the ideal is someone who offers 24/7 support.

Local versus international hosting

Often you will find overseas hosting is the cheapest option. For Australian and New Zealand organisations, local hosting companies can be outrageously expensive and lean on features compared with their US counterparts.

Overseas hosting is a good and cost-effective option, but be mindful that the different time zones can mean support may not be available when you need it; that scheduled maintenance at their quiet times might coincide with your busy time; that Sunday evening in the United States is the start of the work week in New Zealand and Australia; and that it is difficult to settle any disputes when the host is in another country.

PHP scripting

PHP, or personal home page, scripting services are the base of many of the internet's basic tools, particularly the open source programs that are becoming the standard for most online services. Any hosting service you have must offer PHP services or you will find the flexibility and growth of the site will be limited.

Strangely, quite a few providers don't offer this in many of their plans, which locks your site into custom tools or static HTML, the basic language of the web. These options aren't the best, as they lock you out of using the web's standard tools and will cost you time, money and irritation as your business grows.

Email

Any decent service will include email services with at least several gigabytes of storage and a dozen or so addresses. Many services now offer unlimited email addresses as part of their hosting packages, and this is the preferred way to run your site, as it gives you the flexibility to deal with evolving business demands.

Other included services

Good web hosting companies will include various free and add-on services, such as Simple Scripting or Fantastico installations, which give you easy-to-install accessories. Some of those accessories should include Wordpress installation, anti-spam protection and shopping carts. Many good providers offer easy ways to install these tools.

Reliability

The key characteristic of a hosting company to consider is its reliability. If your site is down then you don't have a web presence, so an unreliable host is a lousy deal, regardless of how cheap it is.

Some providers will give their uptime figures, which purport to show how long their systems run without interruption. Treat these figures with caution, as they are prone to exaggeration and the less ethical providers will be somewhat economical with the truth.

Price

Most pricing deals are based on fees for the month or the year. Often deals for annual hosting can be very competitive if you're prepared to commit to 12 months' hosting or more. Usually these deals are upfront payments, so make sure you are comfortable with the stability of the provider before you agree to them.

Another aspect to consider with monthly payments is that missing a monthly payment can leave your site offline. A forgotten transfer or declined credit card can stop your website and interrupt your business.

If you do make a poor decision with a hosting company, all isn't lost, as it's relatively easy to move services. As the owner of your business's domain name, you can point the internet to another provider that you have an account with and it will take, at most, 12 hours to change. Usually the new service is happy to walk you through the process.

However, it's best to find a good service in the first place, as a good web host will make your online presence a lot easier to manage. It will also help your business's reputation for service and reliability.

Conclusion

With your domain chosen and your hosting service set up, you're now ready to choose what type of software, or platform, you want your business to run on. This is discussed further in chapter 9.

Checklist

> Are the prices charged within your budget?

> Does the host have a responsive sales team?

> Does the host provide support services in the hours when you are likely to need them?

> How many email addresses will be available?

> What are the data allowances provided?

> Is PHP scripting available?

> Does the host have an easy-to-use control panel for when you need to make changes to your website?

Chapter 9
Site platforms

With the basics of domain and hosting services settled, the next step to consider in developing your business's website is deciding what it will look like and how it will run—and that depends on the software, known as the platform, that you choose to run your website.

For most people the software their website runs on is a boring topic. However, this is an important choice that will determine the look of your online presence and how much effort and money you will have to put into maintaining and updating the site. One thing is clear—the option you choose should never become an issue for your visitors. The choice you make will affect the look of the site and how easy it is for you to update it or to hire a different website designer, as different platforms offer different options and the ease of updating also varies.

As discussed in chapter 8, on choosing a hosting provider, the choices come down to a number of open source and proprietary programs, with the PHP (personal home page) scripting language being the essential tool in many options. I prefer to use open source tools, as this gives website owners more control. So the focus in this chapter is Wordpress (discussed briefly in step 1). This chapter also looks at some of the other open source options.

Geek wars

Nothing sets geeks off like a good battle over standards, so whichever choice you make be prepared to be criticised by your web designer nephew, system architect neighbour or IT consultant friends.

Most consultants in the industry choose one platform over another for good reasons, but those reasons may not be the right solutions for your business.

When consulting experts on which platform they recommend, always keep in mind that they will have some bias towards a particular option. This is human and understandable—I have a bias towards Wordpress, believing it meets the needs of most businesses. This is another reason for getting a second or third opinion before making a choice.

Proprietary programs include the various Microsoft services, as well as Google's Blogger (see step 1), and various combined hosting and publishing platforms, such as Squarespace.

Proprietary platforms

The term proprietary platform or proprietary software means one that is locked into a single commercial supplier. Microsoft's Office, Exchange and Sharepoint products are good examples of proprietary packages.

Being locked into one commercial supplier has advantages, particularly that support tends to be more professional and focused. The downside is that if the vendor loses interest in the product or you have a falling out with them it is difficult to change providers. You may also find support difficult to find for less popular or declining proprietary services.

This isn't to say there aren't some good proprietary suppliers, including services like Blogger and Squarespace. The most popular one for smaller businesses is Microsoft's Sharepoint, which is included in most of the Microsoft business server platforms. However, most organisations that adopt Sharepoint tend to underestimate the amount of work required to set it up properly. You also need to spend money on buying and setting up a server as this software doesn't come with the normal Microsoft Windows or Microsoft Office packages.

For big business, there are dozens of high-end, expensive systems that meet the needs of large corporations and government departments. Given that this book is about getting your organisation's site running quickly and inexpensively, we're not going to spend any time on them here. If you are considering using an Enterprise system, for instance, you should invest in suitably qualified, and expensive, consultants.

Shopify

For businesses wanting to set up online stores, Shopify is one of the easiest and quickest ways to set up an e-commerce website. The service, which also acts as a hosting company, allows you to use a range of different templates and happily uses your own domain name.

Shopify charges a tiered monthly fee, along with a percentage based on sales transactions, which reduces in line with the higher subscription plans. While it is a proprietary platform, it does offer various plug-ins that allow you to link to other services and local payment gateways offering merchant credit card services and PayPal.

To create a quick, out-of-the-box e-commerce site with minimal fuss and stress, Shopify is a good option, although high-growth businesses might quickly hit some limitations. Given that you're locked into hosting with Shopify, you may hit some of the problems discussed in chapter 8.

Squarespace

Also combining hosting and content management, Squarespace is a proprietary hosting company that does all-in-one websites, providing templates, design features and advanced plug-ins for services like mailing lists and e-commerce. In many ways it's the industrial, high-powered version of the Weebly package discussed in step 1.

For most businesses, Squarespace can get your website running for less than $15 per month, with service fees ranging from $10 to $40 a month depending on the features you choose and how long you sign up for. The Squarespace screen (see figure 9.1) is fairly spartan, but it is easy to update.

Blogger

Part of the Google empire, Blogger started as a personal web log service. Today you can set a Blogger site to look like a professional and businesslike website for free. If you have registered your domain through a registrar, as described in step 2, then adding it to your Blogger site is free.

Being Google, the company provides a heap of free features and services, such as visitor analytics, plug-ins and templates, but it doesn't provide much support. The service is fairly easy to use but customisation requires some understanding of what you are doing.

Blogger was discussed in more detail in step 1 for its free features. Blogger tends to be best for a small, new business.

Figure 9.1: Squarespace configuration page

Open source content management systems

Open source software is generally the best choice on the Net because the data tends to be portable across all the major platforms; you don't get locked out of your data; and thousands of people on the Net can support you.

A common misconception is that open source is free. While that's often the case, it isn't necessarily so. The basic rule of open source software is that if you make a change to the software, you have to share the program with the world.

Because the web is largely based on open source software, it has become the standard way of doing things. For businesses this means more flexibility.

There are dozens of open source content management system (CMS) platforms, but the big three are Joomla, Drupal and Wordpress, the last being by far the most popular.

Wordpress

Of all the open source platforms, Wordpress is the most popular and flexible. While the advanced features can get complex and you may need a specialist to set up and manage them, it offers a quick and easy way to get online.

Wordpress was discussed as free software in step 1, but it comes into its own when it is hosted on another service, where features such as additional plug-in software and customisable templates become available. Along with its huge following of designers and tech support, one of the big attractions of Wordpress is the thousands of layout templates available. Some of these have to be paid for, while many are free and almost all can be customised to a business's specific needs.

Wordpress themes

One of Wordpress's biggest advantages is the vast range of themes, or templates, on offer. With more than a thousand approved free themes and hundreds of premium themes it's possible to run a site without ever buying a design.

In step 2 we looked at the themes selection for the hosted version of Wordpress. The full version offers a much bigger range of themes (see figure 9.2), along with the option to manually install themes from outside Wordpress.

Figure 9.2: Wordpress themes screen

Selecting and installing a theme is straightforward. Go to the *Install themes* page, search through the various options and, once you find a theme you like among the 1300 free ones available, you can install it simply by clicking 'Install' and, once the template has installed, clicking 'Activate'.

It is possible to install a template from outside Wordpress, and thousands of paid themes are available from professional developers. They generally offer improved features and support services, although setting them up requires some knowledge of how your hosting service works and is probably best left to a consultant if you want to go that way.

Themes can be customised and it's worthwhile hiring an experienced Wordpress developer to tweak your site to make it continue to work well as the business grows. For a startup business, the free templates, coupled with some standard plug-ins, will do most of what's required for a small enterprise.

Template traps

One of the traps with free Wordpress templates that you might find outside the official site is that some aren't quite what they seem to be. They can include spyware and other malicious pieces of computer code. The danger with these sites is that once you have installed them, they can be tracking your users or even installing viruses and hijacking passwords from visitors to your website.

Some unscrupulous web merchants also do a good trade in selling older templates that aren't compatible with later versions of Wordpress or have known bugs in them.

Generally it's a good idea to do a bit of research before downloading a Wordpress theme—free or paid—that you have discovered on the web. Have a look at the name of the theme and designer, then search for other versions or user reports on them.

Trusting your gut feelings is always good on the web, as well: If you are uneasy about anything you find online, be it Wordpress themes, free downloads or offers of Nigerian fortunes, then don't go ahead with it.

Plug-ins

The other big attraction for Wordpress is the huge range of plug-ins—mini programs that run within the website. In early 2011 more than 13 000 plug-ins were available, ranging from shopping cart applications through to newsletter subscriptions and mini-arcade games.

Most web services now have a plug-in that connects into Wordpress, such as the Shopify application. This makes it easy to integrate features into a Wordpress-based site. Because almost every Web 2.0 provider, from Google to specialist payment gateways, has plug-ins, Wordpress is a compelling argument for most webmasters.

Adding plug-ins to a Wordpress site is ridiculously simple. It's a matter of going to the plug-ins section of the configuration page (see figure 9.3) and clicking on 'Add new' and then searching for the type of plug-in required.

Figure 9.3: Wordpress plug-in page

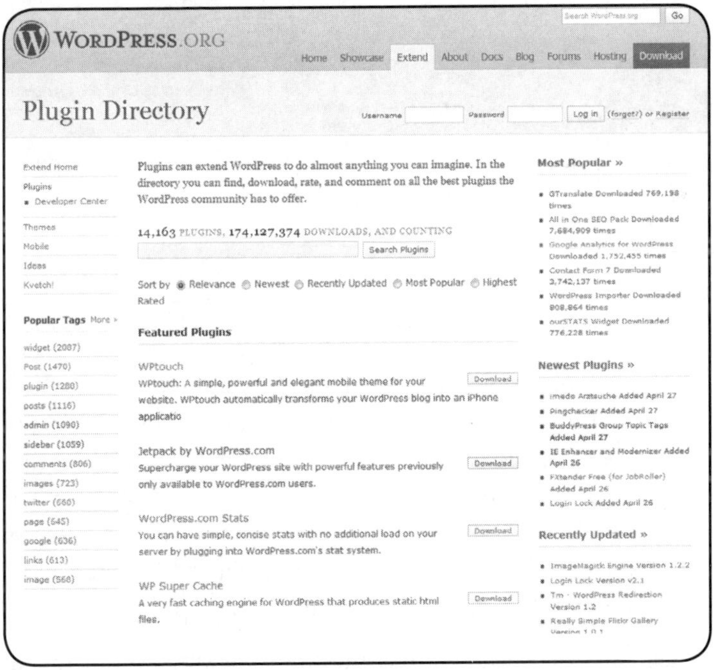

You can check the quality of a Wordpress plug-in by clicking on the 'Details' link, which opens a mini review of the application (see figure 9.4). The details will describe the features and purpose of the plug-in and will also show the version and number of times it has been downloaded. A version greater than 1.0 is best, as many developers have beta, or test, versions numbered less than 1.0, such as .85 or .93. The more downloads there are, the better.

Figure 9.4: Wordpress plug-in details

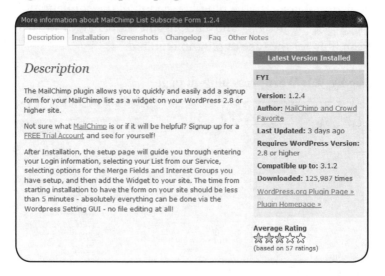

The quality of the plug-in (or app) is also reflected in the review section on the Wordpress website, which gives a star rating of up to five stars and shows the number of votes. While a higher star rating is good, note the number of votes, as a five star–rated plug-in with two votes probably reflects the wishful thinking of the developer and his mum. It's far more likely a four star–rated plug-in with 500 votes is a better, more stable product.

Once you have installed the plug-in by clicking on the 'Install now' link, you may have to configure the plug-in. Depending on the service, it could be something simple, such as a password, or it might involve complex security and identity keys. This will vary with the plug-in.

If the plug-in will display on your pages—many of them run functions behind the scenes, like the Akismet spam checker in figure 9.5—then you can use the 'Widget' setting in 'Appearances' to drag the plug-in's screen into the right position on your site.

Figure 9.5: Wordpress widget layout

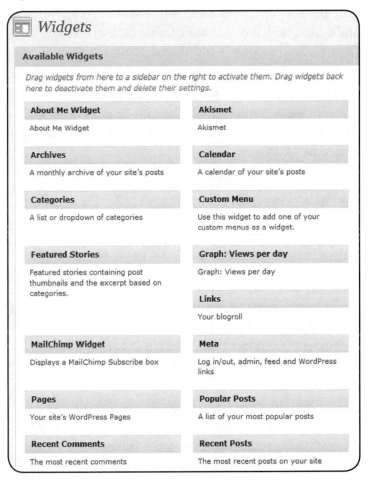

Joomla

Another open source CMS is Joomla, which is often used for sites requiring a higher level of customisation than Wordpress. Because it requires a higher understanding and level of software skills than Wordpress, it's generally best not to play with it unless you have at least a moderate understanding of the PHP scripting language or you're prepared to pay someone who has.

Like Wordpress, Joomla has a range of both paid and free plug-ins and templates that can be downloaded, installed and customised. Joomla's strength has been in its community features, such as forums and shared photo albums.

In recent times, Joomla's adoption has been falling away as Wordpress has become more robust, scalable and suitable for multiple users. While Joomla can still be a good choice, it's value for your business will depend on the consultant you hire to build the site.

Drupal

The other major CMS is Drupal, which has established itself as the CMS for large-scale, high-traffic sites.

If you have the high traffic and demanding requirements that a Drupal site works best for, then you will be best served hiring an experienced consultant who knows how to design for this platform. Drupal can be expensive to run because of its complexity, but if your business requires the kind of robust performance Drupal offers, then it's an investment worth making.

Drupal also offers plug-ins and templates, like Wordpress and Joomla, but they are less common and require a far higher level of customisation than the other two options. Generally

Drupal is a preferred option when you have, or are prepared to buy in, technical capacity.

Conclusion

There are many other platforms for running websites, although Wordpress is becoming the tool of choice for most businesses because it offers the basic features that most businesses need and much of the basic setup can be done by a business.

This isn't to say that other specific tools, such as Shopify, Drupal, Sharepoint or Squarespace, aren't right for some businesses. It's worthwhile investigating the options if you have specific requirements for user access or shopping carts or expect a lot of traffic to your website.

Once you have decided on the software to support your website, you are ready to develop the distinctive look of your own website, and that's the subject of step 4 and the following chapters.

Checklist

➤ Which content platforms are common in your industry?

➤ How quickly do you want to get your website online?

➤ What level of technical expertise do you have, or are you prepared to pay for?

➤ Do you have any special requirements for your website, such as shopping carts?

➤ What functions do you expect on your website?

➤ Have you asked other businesses about their experiences with different platforms?

➤ What platforms does your hosting company support?

Step 4
The look

Chapter 10
Designing a website

Once you have decided on the basics—name, domain, hosting service and software—it's time to turn your attention to the look of your website. Over the next two chapters we will focus on how to achieve the look you want.

Design is probably the element people notice most when they first encounter our business online. Although we often underestimate the importance of design, it is also an aspect of the online presence that can paralyse a new business for months, as the owners quibble over the many fonts, colours and layouts available.

In the days of print we were locked into design decisions for months or even years until we ran out of business cards or saved enough money to spend on another print run. The advantage of the web is that our designs and logos can evolve without great cost or embarrassment. It is important that the design of your website is consistent with the rest of your business. You need to consider all the elements you use, including business cards, signage and anything else the public sees.

Ideally everything would be custom designed by a designer, but most of us simply don't have the budget for that. Luckily we have some other options. This isn't to say that free is best — you will get far superior results hiring a skilled designer than any free or purchased template will provide — but for getting a site up quickly and cheaply, buying off the shelf is a better solution. This chapter focuses on using and customising templates.

Templates versus designers

Many businesses have been turned off the internet by expensive web design prices. In the early days of the web, designing a site was a long, labour-intensive project, where bills could easily run into the tens, or even hundreds, of thousands of dollars. Often relationships between web developers and business owners ended poorly, as they argued over bills, definitions and misunderstandings about the amount of work required to do a project.

Large businesses and governments still spend vast amounts on their sites, while today most small businesses use templates — standard designs bought cheaply or obtained for free — from brokers and web designers. For businesses watching their pennies in the early stages, an off-the-shelf free or paid-for template is usually adequate, although without any customisation the organisation's identity may also get a little lost.

To keep a consistent brand, it's usually necessary to do some customisation of the templates to get the site right, and that's where most web designers now step in. Usually a designer can make some basic changes to the look and feel of a template or website without the owner spending thousands.

Web designers still have an important role, but most small businesses don't rely on them to the extent they did some years back. This makes the design process far cheaper, quicker and more flexible. Nonetheless, you should always consider the services of a good designer if the budget allows for it.

Choosing a web designer

As in any successful business, good web designers listen to their customers. On the first meeting with a designer, they should be quiet and listen to what your needs and requirements are. If they come in telling you what to do before you have even explained what you want, then you know the relationship won't go well.

Keep in mind that your designer doesn't have to be local: it's quite possible to hire a designer from anywhere in the world and have all your meetings and conversations over the internet. Just remember that if you hire very cheap workers from developing economies, their standard of work and the supervision required may make what looks like a cheaper worker more expensive than an experienced one in your home country.

Before calling a designer, have a look at their own website. Is their site clear, well designed and looking good? If they can't do a good job for themselves, it's hard to have confidence that they will do a good job for you.

Web designers will have testimonials and references on their own websites. It's worthwhile calling some of the

> businesses the designer claims to have worked for to check that they actually did do the work and the quoted praise is real: it's depressingly common to find people in the web and IT industries lying about the work they have done in the past.
>
> Finally, watch the quotes. A good proposal will be clear on the work that will be done and when it will be delivered. Many quotations are vague, which is a recipe for misunderstanding and disputes when bills arrive.

A good web designer will still be a great help for your site as it develops, and they should be a valued part of your business team. However, establishing the basics through the use of a template is how most new ventures start their web presence.

Choosing a template

The templates available to you will depend upon the platform you have chosen to run your site. If you've chosen Squarespace, Blogger, Weebly or another proprietary platform, you'll be largely restricted to the templates available there, although some of them allow you to modify the look and feel to varying extents.

The advantage with choosing open source platforms is the range of templates is far broader. Wordpress has more than 1300 free themes available on their site, such as the Arras theme in figure 10.1, with thousands more premium and free ones available on the web. Many of these offer licences that allow you to modify the themes, and a lot of the developers actually encourage their customers to make their own changes and customisations.

Figure 10.1: example of a Wordpress theme

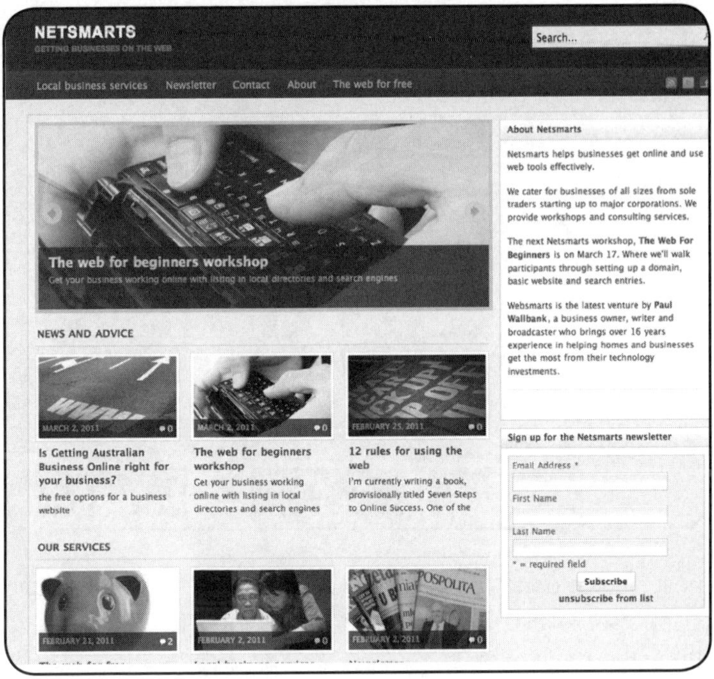

In choosing a template (see figure 10.2, overleaf), you'll be looking for a theme that's close to your business branding, even if only the colour is similar. The good thing is that most themes can be customised, although this is where the web developer might come in.

When choosing a Wordpress theme, you will need to look at the various features available. At the very least, the theme or template needs to support the latest version of Wordpress, or whichever platform you're using, and be able to run plug-ins that add various features (see step 3).

You should also consider the layout of your website. There is a basic layout that web designers have found works well for

Figure 10.2: Wordpress themes directory

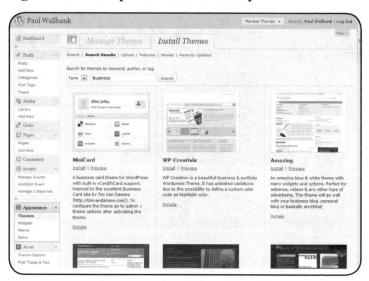

most sites and viewers. The standard layout for the first page visitors see — usually called the landing, or index, page — is discussed in chapter 11.

Shopping around

One of the best ways of figuring out what theme is right for your business is to have a prowl on the web. If you see a site that looks good, go to the bottom of the screen, where you will usually see a credit for the web designer. If the website has used a free or premium theme, it's good manners for the owner to acknowledge the template and its designer with a link to their site. You can then visit the designer's page and see what they have for offer, either free or as a paid-for template.

Often the free templates are available for your platform directly using the built-in theme installer. This is particularly true in Wordpress, which offers over 1300 free templates directly from their site.

A warning on templates

While templates are great for the cost-conscious business, there are some risks in installing free templates from any source, as they include computer codes that can cause problems for visitors to your business's website.

Some templates are simply out of date or poorly written, which can cause browsers to crash, while others may deliberately contain code to steal visitors' information or infect their computers with viruses and other nasties.

It's best to download templates only from sites you trust, so generally steer clear of websites offering freebies and buy templates only from sites that have a clear bill of health once you have checked them using a web search on the site or its products.

The basic layout

In choosing a template, look for the colours and layout you intend to use for your website. Although you can change them later, it's easier to get the general look and feel of your business roughly correct at the very beginning.

When choosing a layout, one choice is the one-, two- and three- column format. Each format has its own benefits, although web-surfers tend to prefer the two- and three-column formats, as they break up the page and let you get more information out while not allowing your web pages to look too cluttered.

Watch the fold

An idea that has entered the web world from the old medium of print is the fold. In newspaper terms, the fold was where a large-format, or broadsheet, newspaper was folded over so it would fit on the news stand. On the web, the fold is the point on the page where most people would have to scroll down to read it.

Conventional wisdom is that web-surfers are lazy and don't want to scroll if they can avoid it, so your key information and calls to action have to be towards the top of a page: there is no point in having them at the bottom if no-one can see them or be bothered to scroll to them.

Hidden information

Behind the scenes on a web page there's information called metadata that explains what the page is to search engines, web browsers and other computers. This normally isn't seen by visitors to a website but it's a crucial part of how the web and, particularly, search engines work.

Every site has its own metadata that describes what the organisation does, the type of site it is and where it's hosted, among a lot of other information. In turn, each page has its own description of the content on it and within each page individual links and other data have their own little explanations.

All of this metadata is important as it helps search engines figure out how relevant your page is. Title, keyword, description and alt tags — mini descriptions that accompany pictures on websites — all need to be filled in when you are creating a page so the site is as accessible as possible for both search engines and people who are visually impaired. In step 5, which looks at metadata in more detail, we discuss search engine optimisation and being found on the web.

Basic customisation

When you use a web template there will be some basic settings that have to be customised regardless of how standard the design is. These will include descriptions, some of the metadata, along with things like adding your business name and byline, which you should fill in immediately so the site doesn't look silly or confuse visitors.

Many templates will include some images and links to services such as Twitter and Facebook that will either be dead or point to the designer's accounts. You will need to go through these and modify the settings, the location of which varies with every theme, so they are either disabled or send visitors to your social media accounts.

The favicon

One of the quirky little features in websites is the favicon — the little graphic that sits next to the website address at the top of the browser screen. While many sites leave it blank, you can configure your site to show your logo, which helps the business brand.

The favicon measures just 16 × 16 pixels (4 mm by 4 mm) and usually has the .ico suffix, although any common graphics format like .jpg or .gif will do. A number of do-it-yourself favicon tools are available, and you can even download a ready-made one (see the *eBusiness* website at <www.ebusinessbook.com.au>).

Generally, however, it's best to create an icon that's built on your logo so that it enhances your brand rather than use a generic icon.

Setting up the favicon may involve making some deep-down changes to the theme or template you use. In Wordpress a number of plug-ins and built-in theme features will do all the changes for you, and sites such as Squarespace and Weebly offer a customised icon as part of their premium services, although you will have to pay a few dollars a month for them.

Add-on features

Key ingredients in all modern websites are the little add-on programs — variously known as add-ons, widgets, gadgets and plug-ins — that enhance a website's features. These can add functions, such as calendars, connections to other sites and popular posts, and automate many of the search engine optimisation services and other time-consuming tasks.

Some of the add-ons, such as the various tracking plug-ins, search engine optimisation and Twitter tools, operate in the background and carry out administrative functions. Others add features to the website, such as easy newsletter signup forms, contact pages and events calendars.

While Wordpress has more than 13 000 plug-ins (see step 3) and other platforms come close to that, most do have the basic range of search engine optimisation, shopping cart and other add-ons needed for running a site. Blogger, as shown in figure 10.3, had more than 1100 in early 2011.

It's best to look at other websites and decide what features you would like to see on your pages. Typical plug-ins installed on a site are recent post lists, newsletter subscription and popular posts. A lot of features are available and it's worthwhile spending a few hours deciding which are right for you.

While most plugs-ins, gadgets or add-ons are free, some will work only if you have an account with the service provider, which may be a paid-for premium service. A good example is the pretty much essential Akismet service, which monitors your site and email for spam: it offers both a free service for personal use and a paid commercial service.

Figure 10.3: Blogger gadget (plug-in) search

Various plug-ins have different levels of complexity and require varying amounts of effort to set up. Some of the more sophisticated payment plug-ins and those with high levels of security, for instance, require some fairly high level knowledge and information to install. Others, such as Wordpress's 'About me 3000' plug-in (see figure 10.4), let you run loose and be creative in describing you or your business.

Figure 10.4: 'About me 3000' Wordpress plug-in

One of the great things about most of the plug-ins is that they can be dragged and dropped around the screen, making it very easy to rearrange or add plug-ins. The Blogger layout screen in figure 10.5 shows a typical layout and how various features can be updated, moved or disabled.

Figure 10.5: the Blogger layout screen

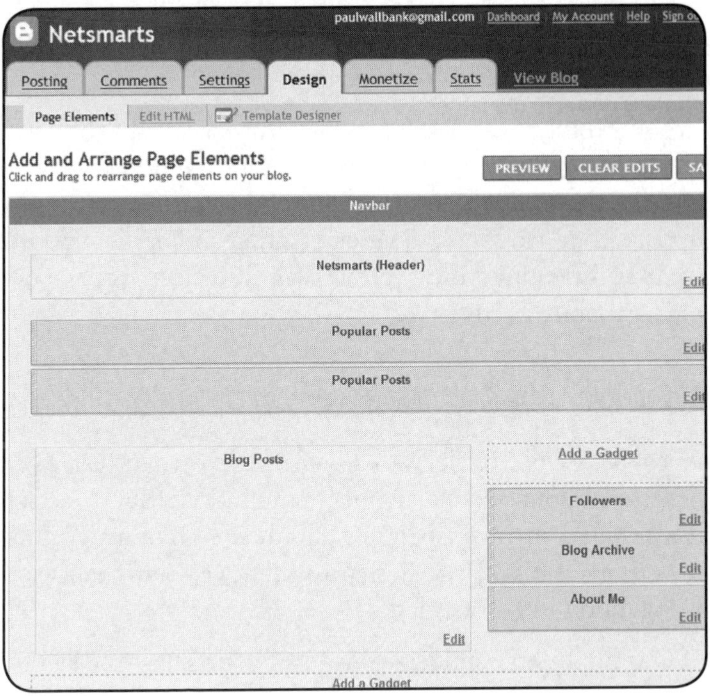

Keep it clean and simple

A trap with all these wonderful tools is that it's tempting to put too much information on the screen. Don't try to throw too much information at the visitor: too much text and too many links confuse the message and clutter the page. Make sure the essentials are there, but don't go overboard.

Keep it fresh

In step 7 we discuss adding fresh and interesting content in detail, but at this stage it's enough to say you should be adding something every week or so to keep the search engines interested in your site.

If your business relies solely on web sales, then you will have to keep it up to date far more often. Typical news is going to be special offers, new products and topics that might be of special interest to your customers.

Keeping things fresh also feeds into any social media tools you are using. Most sites have a widget, or mini application, which is really the same thing as a plug-in, that will automatically update your Facebook, Twitter or other online networking feed, so updating your website will also keep your social media channels active.

Search engine obsession

Since the rise of Google, web designers and owners have been obsessed about search engine optimisation (SEO), which has resulted in their spending inordinate amounts of time reworking text and site design to improve their chances of being found by web-surfers.

SEO is important, and all elements of your site—the layout, content and the hidden metadata—form part of what the search engines and directories are looking for. SEO and the other strategies for being found on the web are discussed in step 5.

Conclusion

While you can hire a designer—and spend a lot of money—to create the perfect website for your business, it's also an easy matter for business owners to use online templates and customise them to reflect their business. In the next chapter we'll look at the design of specific features and pages on your website, from the home page to headers and footers.

Checklist

> ➤ Does the chosen template look like your brand?

> ➤ Can the chosen template be customised to your needs?

> ➤ Are plug-ins, add-ons and widgets supported by your template?

> ➤ Is the template suitable for the latest version of your platform?

> ➤ Did the template come from a trusted source?

> ➤ Have you reviewed the plug-ins you will need?

> ➤ What templates are other sites in your industry using?

Chapter 11

The content

With the look of your website now established, probably through the use of a template, it's time to develop the individual pages that will attract customers and add essential information about your business.

Your own business website is a chance for you to shine. The pages on your site are all yours to work with and, as long as you aren't saying anything illegal or defamatory, you are free to portray your business in whatever way you want it to be seen. Every other medium, such as television or newspapers, has some sort of restriction on what, when and where you can do things: on your own website you are totally in control of your message.

Having full control of the medium gives a business owner great power, although most of us find that power is intimidating, so we tend to shy away from making the best use of a site. That's a shame as we can do a lot on a web page.

While we can say whatever we like, there are common layouts and content that internet users and search engines have come to expect. While you can buck convention—particularly if you have a funky web designer—you can expect the average user to become quickly confused and go elsewhere if you get too clever.

In the early days of your site it's best to stick to the basics in your web design and site layout. The first step is to choose the pages you wish to create for your website.

Home page

Also known as the index page, this is the entrance to your website. If someone types yourbusiness.com.au into a search engine, the index page is what they will see. It needs to grab the visitor's attention and convey the most important information about the business.

Figure 11.1 shows an example of a recommended page layout, including the preferred elements and typical placing.

Figure 11.1: anatomy of a page layout

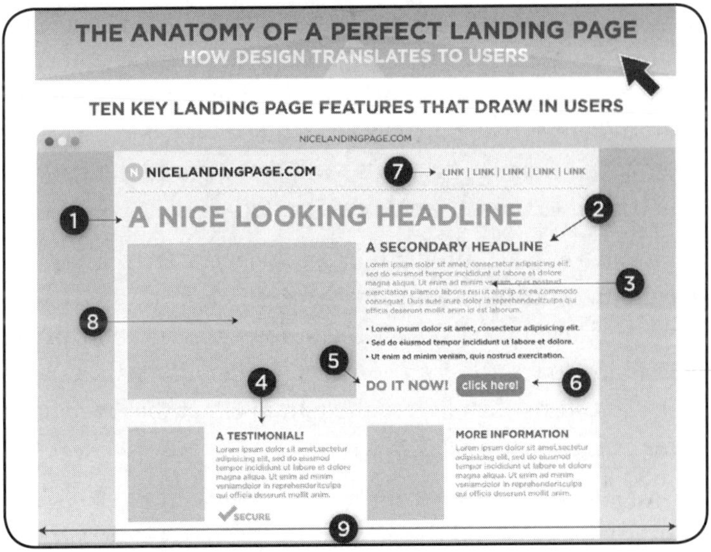

Source: courtesy of Formstack.com.

While it isn't necessary for your home page to be identical to the example, a similar layout is a good place to start, particularly in the early days of your site.

Ideally the home page will offer a tantalising but short description of what you do, what products you sell and, if you have a physical shop, your opening hours and locations. All of this summarises the detail you will have on other pages.

About us

A commonly missed opportunity is the *About us* page. Too often this features a bland, anonymous description of the organisation's 'commitment to service' or other blah that sounds like a 1990s mission statement.

The *About us* page is an opportunity for your business to shine. This is the time to boast about the awards you have won and the great products you have developed and to also show the human side of your organisation. If you sponsor a local sports team, you're a member of the local chamber of commerce or you donated to the school building appeal, tell your audience. Not only does this make you look like the good, local business, but it also will help your ranking in the search engines, which we discuss in step 5.

If you have been profiled or interviewed in the media, make sure you have links to those articles or video clips. If the publication has taken them down, see if you can get permission to use them on your site and set up separate pages for each feature, then link to them from either the *About us* or home pages.

Customers love to hear your story so make sure your *About us* page tells it. Why did you start the business? How did you became the best plumber in Parkes or baker in Ballarat? What are your business triumphs and how have you supported your community. Don't waste an opportunity to tell people why they should come to you. Remember that call to action at the end of it.

Contact information

Give your customers every opportunity to contact you: if you won't let customers talk to you, then there's little point in being on the Net. Give customers a phone number, a physical address (even if it is a post office box) and an email contact form.

Surveys have shown that customers tend to trust businesses that have a street address and a phone number on their website. If you are working from home, it might be worthwhile having a virtual office address—basically a mail drop—for a hundred dollars or so per year that gives you that credibility. Establishing a separate business phone number or having a 1300 number is also a good credibility builder.

If you are using social media, include those links too. Having direct links to the business's Facebook, Twitter, LinkedIn and other services shows you are a serious operation that has gone to the effort of being credible online.

The more ways people have to contact you, the more chance you have of converting them into customers. Today's shoppers are looking for you as much in Facebook as they used to in the Yellow Pages.

News and blogs

Search engines and customers like sites that are regularly updated, so adding a regular news feature or blog posts once every month or so encourages them to come back to your website (for more information, see step 7). For the moment, though, it's enough to say some fresh information posted regularly on your site will help your business.

Your products

You can't forget your products and a website gives you the opportunity to be generous about what you supply and do. By going into detail about the products, while not giving too much away about your services, you can address most customer questions and improve your page rankings with the search engines.

While it's probably not feasible for the beginning business to list every product, which is time consuming even if you have chosen a dedicated shopping platform like Shopify (see step 3) as you have to fill in the description for every line you carry, it is still worthwhile having dedicated pages describing the details of your popular and most profitable lines.

The elements of a page

While every business's website is different, to reflect the unique character and proposition of the business, a number of factors common to every website make it informative for customers and useful to your business. The elements of each page also need to be consistent, so that visitors aren't puzzled by different layouts on each page.

Page title

The title of the page should tell the visitor who the business is and what it does in a clear, concise way that hopefully entertains and piques the customer's curiosity. There are also search engine optimisation benefits in having a good page title.

The headlines

Just as with newspapers, the reader's—and the search engines'—attention is grabbed by a short, interesting headline. Many websites trying to sell online will ask a question, offer a list or challenge the reader with a question or provocative statement.

Regardless of which type of title you use, it needs to be related to the content of the page or post. If it's irrelevant, it will turn readers off your site and they will go elsewhere.

Strong call to action

Your site, and each post, should have a call to action. What do you want readers to do? The site should make it easy for customers to call your phone number, download your ebook or click the 'Buy now' button.

Make what you're offering obvious: if it's not clear the visitor will probably give up and go elsewhere. Whatever you do, don't get the customer stuck in a loop or confuse them with inconsistent page layouts.

Consistent organisation

Every website needs a menu, often called a navigation bar, that helps readers find their way around the site. There will be different options on setting up a menu bar depending upon the template or platform you choose to use.

Usually the navigation elements are placed across the top of the page or down the right-hand side of the page. Whichever you choose, make sure they are consistent, as having the menu in different locations on various pages will confuse visitors.

Allow comments

One thing that will keep your site fresh is offering your customers the ability to add or update comments. By enabling this feature, you will give clients the opportunity to engage with you.

While a comments page can be time consuming and is not without risks (as we'll discuss in step 7), it will allow people to talk to you and show your business as being an open, friendly authority in your field of expertise.

Testimonials

If you can fit them in on each page, a few testimonials from genuine users are a great way to give visitors confidence about your business and services. A separate page for testimonials can also work, but sprinkling them through the site tends to work best.

The trap of false testimonials

A common, and unethical, trick is to put fake testimonials on your website extolling the virtues of your business. Not only is this poor manners, it's also illegal.

In early 2011 a company that sold allergy cures was prosecuted for allowing false testimonials on their Facebook page after they had already been ordered to take down fake stories from their website.

If you are going to put up testimonials from happy customers, or even staff for your recruitment pages, then you need to make sure records of the original testimonial have been kept so you can prove they are genuine should a dispute arise.

Another way of engendering confidence is by including recognised brand names of products you supply. If you link out to those supplier sites you will also be adding credibility to your brand.

Citing previous companies you have supplied or worked for can also establish credibility, but be careful that you don't overdo this by being too enthusiastic about citing clients who you didn't work for directly. Many small operations look foolish when clients find out the work with big corporations meant only that the business owner had been employed as an intern when they were at university or once worked part time in the call centre.

Naturally awards and certifications are something you should be proud of, so don't be shy in publicising anything your business has earned. If possible include them on the front page and make a fuss about them in the *About us* page.

Of course, if a celebrity or a prominent local identity has recommended you, then don't hold that back either. Make sure their endorsement is prominently displayed for all your visitors.

Images and video

The web is a visual medium and lively, relevant images help the reader understand your story. When using images or videos make sure the name you give them describes the picture or video. Also make good use of alt tags that contain descriptions of images and links for the search engines and accessibility software, as shown in figure 11.2, overleaf.

Giving names to images and videos that include the most commonly searched for terms is a great way to improve useability and getting the attention of search engines. So if you're a plumber wanting to advertise emergency hot water service repairs, you might want to have a photo of a damaged hot water heater with the name repair_hot_water_tank_ joe_the_plumber.jpg, which will improve the search engine results for your site.

Figure 11.2: a web image attributes page

Similarly the alt tags should have a clear description of what the image or video is, because this helps the search engines and any sight-impaired person visiting your page using accessibility software. The easier you make it for all of your prospective customers, as well as the search engines, the more interest you will get from visitors.

Headers and footers

All web pages have standard information at the top and the bottom of the page. At the top should be your logo, the name of the organisation, a byline and preferably your contact information so that regardless of where your visitor is on your page, they can remember who you are.

At the bottom of each page should be the stuff most of your visitors will find boring—things like legal disclaimers, links to official information, copyright statements, privacy policies and site credits—but which is essential. Don't put these too far up the page as they will only clutter the information you want to get across.

In general the most eye-catching, most profitable and most relevant information should be at the top of the page and above the fold. The further down the page the reader goes, the drier and older the content can be. What your visitor sees in the first few seconds could be the difference between their staying to investigate or leaving your site.

Checklist

➤ Is the home page clear and concise?

➤ Does the home page have your contact details and opening hours?

➤ Is the *About us* page informative and does it describe the business accurately?

➤ Are all the pages consistent in layout and look?

➤ Do you have plenty of testimonials scattered around the site?

➤ Are your major products described on the *Products* page?

➤ Is there at least one image on every page?

Chapter 12

Payment options

While having a nice-looking website is very important, for many businesses the reason for being online is to sell products. In this chapter we look at managing payments through your website. Even if you don't want to become an internet millionaire, giving your customers another opportunity to give you money is not a bad thing.

A secure payment system on the Net is one of the trickier areas for any business, as it requires a certain degree of expertise in online security and managing the risk of fraud or data breaches. Because of the complexity and risk involved in the online payment process, I urge businesses to get help from qualified and experienced consultants for this part of their website development. The aim of this chapter is to explain the process and some of the tools available to you as a business owner.

Online payment processing

The best place to start a discussion of online payments is with an explanation of the six steps in the online payments system.

Step 1: the customer order

The first stage in online payment is where consumers complete their orders on your website. This should be done on a secure web page so that the customer's personal information — such as credit card or direct deposit details — is encrypted and can't be intercepted and read by third parties while it is being transferred over the internet.

Step 2: data collection

As the customer fills in the details, the site's shopping cart program gathers the order information into the format that the credit card processing company expects.

Step 3: verification

The shopping cart program then sends the order to the credit card processor through a payment gateway. The credit card processor checks the information to be sure it has everything it needs to process the transaction. It then asks the customer's credit card provider to check that the customer's account is valid and has sufficient funds available to pay the bill.

Step 4: approval

If all goes well the customer's credit card company approves the purchase. If the credit card company declines the charge, it sends a code back to the credit card processor explaining the problem.

Step 5: communication

Once the transaction is approved, the credit card processor tells the shopping cart program if the transaction was successful and the shopping cart program tells the customer if the order was complete and sends the order on to the merchant for delivery of the product or service.

Step 6: delivery and payment

While you deliver the product, the credit card processor starts a funds transfer to the company holding your merchant account for deposit into your bank account. The money is transferred after a certain amount of time to allow time to check for fraud or chargebacks.

This is a fairly cumbersome and complex process, so there are a number of overheads for business, not least in obtaining a merchant facility. This can be tricky and expensive, as banks are reluctant to allow an online business the ability to take credit card sales due to the risks involved. Some businesses have massive dispute rates, which adds to both the bank's and the merchant's costs.

The chargeback

When a customer disputes a transaction, the bank or payment provider carries out a chargeback to the merchant, where the disputed amount is deducted from the business's account.

Disputed transactions are the biggest headache and risk to any business operating online and in some industries the rates of chargeback resulting from credit card fraud are high, which sucks up management time and costs.

One reason the fees charged for carrying out transactions online are so high is credit card companies and banks quite rightly want to reduce chargeback rates. They pass the costs of managing online fraud back to the merchants.

Data security

Another aspect of taking online payment is the business's responsibility for protecting their customers' data, particularly their financial information. For big business and the banks, a standard called the Payment Card Industry Data Security Standard (PCI DSS) has been developed. While the mechanics of the standard are complex, the basic rules for small business are:

→   Don't store any sensitive cardholder data.

→   You must install secure payment systems, such as Point Of Sale terminals and websites.

Should your business lose cardholder details the brand damage can be severe, as you will lose the trust of customers. The banks will also punish you severely, and there can even be prosecutions under various privacy and data protection acts.

The best way to deal with the sensitive and complex field of finding the right consultant for your business is to appoint a qualified consultant to integrate the payment system and shopping cart into your website, leaving you to focus on your business. Appendix B discusses what to look for when seeking help from a consultant.

A large number of organisations offer payment services, but PayPal is the biggest.

PayPal

The most common online payment service is PayPal, which is owned by the internet auction site eBay and operates around the world. While the company works hard to avoid being classified as a bank, it has become the de facto bank for most online businesses.

PayPal's strength comes from its simplification of the six-step payment process, offering a choice of payment methods to customers and the ease of setting up a business account. Naturally the charges vary with the amount of money a business passes through PayPal's service. The highest rate for new businesses is a 30 cent transaction fee plus 2.4 per cent of the amount charged, so fees of $2.70 would be deducted from a $100 payment.

For businesses signing up with PayPal, the process is fairly easy compared with signing up for a bank merchant service, consisting of completing a relatively straightforward form asking for business details and Australian company or business number (ACN or ABN). If you already have signed up for a personal account with PayPal, you can upgrade it to a business account.

Once you have signed up, you can incorporate six different payment methods into your website. Fortunately they all have the same commission structure so you won't be penalised for using one method over another. The different PayPal options are as follows.

PayPal Email Payments

The email payment option is the simplest. When a customer buys off your site, you send them an email with the PayPal payment details and the customer does the rest. Later you check the customer has deposited the money with PayPal before dispatching the goods.

Website Payments Standard

Adding a 'Pay now' button to your website makes things look professional, as well as being simple for customers, who just have to click the button to start the sales process. Incorporating this button requires some knowledge of website editing, although most of the standard web platforms described in step 3 have plug-ins you can use to set up this feature simply.

Express Checkout

One of the most popular functions on higher traffic sites, the checkout function allows customers to choose multiple items, which makes it easier for them to buy from you. This option involves PayPal being able to talk to your website, and there's some programming involved, so setting this up is best done by a professional.

PayPal for Digital Goods

A variation on the express checkout is the digital goods service, which adds features suited to merchants selling downloadable products, such as ebooks, games or music.

PayPal on eBay

If you are running an auction site, the PayPal on eBay service integrates the payment and auction services. It's useful to have the PayPal functions integrated if a large part of your business turnover comes through selling on eBay.

Mass Payment

PayPal's Mass Payment service is suited to businesses that deal with lots of small payments to and from affiliates and agents, or paying customer rewards or rebates.

When the customer pays the money, it is credited to your PayPal account, and you can leave the money here or transfer it to another account. We recommend transferring the money at the earliest possible opportunity and keeping as little as possible on deposit with PayPal.

PayPal problems

One of PayPal's points of difference is their dispute resolution procedures. Unlike the banks, which often simply stop payment on a merchant dispute, PayPal tries to bring the two parties in a dispute together.

While this usually works well, some merchants have found their accounts frozen for extended periods and often have difficulty finding out from PayPal why their account has been stopped and when they will be able to access their funds. This is why we recommend keeping the amount of money sitting in your PayPal account to a bare minimum.

Overall, PayPal is by far the easiest service to use for the small business starting on the Net. It does have its downsides, though, and when you engage a consultant to help you set up your online payment system, you should listen to their views as to whether PayPal is the right choice for your business.

Google Checkout

Probably the biggest international competitor to PayPal is Google's Checkout service. This has the advantage of tying into the suite of Google's other services, making it easy to manage.

Unfortunately Google Checkout is currently available only in the United Kingdom and the United States, which is one of the reasons it is nowhere near as popular as PayPal. For Australian businesses, Google's option isn't viable and it doesn't appear that it will be for some years.

Other payment gateway services

Dozens of services provide payment gateways for websites, ranging from your bank or credit card merchant service to independent third parties.

Choosing your bank to deal with your payment gateway needs is an obvious option, but it's not always a good idea, as most of the bank services are expensive and sometimes not as reliable as a merchant needs. Another disadvantage with using a bank is that you are locked into that bank's platform, which makes things complex if you decide to change banks or payment gateways. Generally it's not a good idea to use the bank's systems directly.

The other option is to use a third party gateway system — some of these do an exceptionally good job of building secure, compliant payment platforms. They have the added advantage of being able to offer merchant services from the various banks at substantially reduced rates. Some of the leading Australian companies in the online payment systems are eWay, eMatters and SecurePay. The links to all of these providers are found on the *eBusiness* website at <www. ebusinessbook.com.au>.

Another reason for choosing a dedicated payment company is that they work hard with banks and software developers to come up with well-designed plug-ins and shopping carts for the various website platforms. Again, your consultant will advise you on what solution they think is best for you.

Shopping cart plug-ins

With the payments sorted out, most websites then have to organise the shopping experience for their visitors. If you have chosen one of the easier PayPal options or Shopify (see step 3), then you probably don't need to worry about a dedicated shopping cart program.

For other platforms, you will need either custom-written code or a plug-in for your site. Many of the payment gateway companies offer plug-ins designed for their services, and all of them cater for the more popular hosting and website platforms discussed in step 3.

Wordpress shopping carts

The most popular three shopping carts on this platform are WP E-Commerce, WP Live Shopping and eShop, and each has its fans and critics. These three are not the only Wordpress options, and by early 2011 there were over a hundred plug-ins available.

Many of the Wordpress shopping carts operate on the freemium model—offering a basic free version with extra features in the paid edition. Generally the paid editions will be better for a business, as reliability and security issues are too important to be left to free services.

Which Wordpress plug-in you choose will again depend on the views of your consultant and the ability of your payment gateway to work with it.

Regardless of what platform, plug-in and payment gateway you use, a shopping cart is a major responsibility. You will need to keep your product descriptions, prices and stock levels up to date just as you would in a physical shop. Very few services are set and forget.

Conclusion

Setting up your website to accept payment from your customers can be a complex business. This is one of the times that an expert will make a real difference to the security and reliability of whatever service you choose.

Having set up the look of your website, created the essential pages and organised payment services, you will want to be able to measure what's happening on your site. The internet offers many ways of measuring your progress, and this is the subject of the next chapter.

Checklist

➤ Have you checked the background, online presence and publications of the e-commerce consultant you are considering hiring?

➤ Are you taking steps to ensure you are not saving customers' credit card or banking details anywhere on your site?

➤ Have you ensured any payment service you use is PCI DSS compliant?

➤ Are all of your e-commerce services using strong passwords?

➤ Are you keeping your product descriptions and prices up to date?

➤ Do you have a routine that ensures you regularly sweep funds out of any PayPal accounts you hold?

Chapter 13

Tracking progress

There's an old saying in business that 'you can't manage what you can't measure'. Managers in many parts of small and startup businesses rely on gut feeling to make decisions, because many aspects of business are hard to measure. Luckily, the online world isn't one of those areas, as measuring your site's effectiveness is quite easy.

Once your website has been set up you will want to know that it works and is achieving what you want from it. Fortunately the web offers many tools, many of them free, for the small business owner to track what's working and where the customers are going. This chapter looks in depth at a few of the paid and free options for keeping an eye on your visitors.

Google webmaster tools

Google has an impressive array of free tools as part of its Google Analytics and Webmaster tools. You can retrieve an impressive amount of data using these tools, including tracking visitors by their location, how long they have stayed on your site and the number of pages they have opened. A summary of the key statistics that you can get through Google Analytics is shown in the shaded box. These figures will give you an idea of the performance of your website.

Google Analytics is a valuable tool and a must-have for every website owner. Because it's free, there's no question you should be using it. The analytics *Welcome* page is shown in figure 13.1 (on p. 159), and down the left hand-side of the screen you'll find the statistics grouped by their headings.

The key website performance statistics

A mind-numbing number of statistics are available for the webmaster, but the key ones worth watching are the following.

- *Visits*. Records how many visits your site had over the last month.

- *Page views*. The number of pages opened by the visitors.

- *Pages/visits*. A simple division of the number of pages divided by the number of visitors to give the average number of pages visitors opened.

- *Bounce rate*. How many visitors left after seeing the first page. Unlike the above stats, the lower this number is the better.

- *Average time on site*. How long each visitor spent on your site. Again, the longer stays are more desireable.

- *Percentage new visits*. The proportion of new visitors of your total online traffic.

It's important not to stress too much about these statistics or read too much into them. For instance, while a longer time on site and multiple page views is usually considered good, it may also indicate visitors are finding the site confusing or finding it hard to locate what they want on the site.

Generally, though, these basic statistics help you measure how well the site is doing, so it's worthwhile watching the trends for each figure.

Google also allows you to track more than one website, so if you have more than one site, you can just add it to the control panel. Open one of them and you will find the broad range of data available.

In the *Analytics* screen, you'll find a wealth of information on who visited you and where they went. The initial dashboard view shows the broader trends in visits and the global locations of your visitors.

The Google Analytics tool is worth keeping tabs on as its comprehensive nature lets you customise the tracking process; and the *Intelligence* page lets you set up alerts for certain usage patterns and behaviour triggers, which can be useful if you're testing new pages or products.

The 'Visitors' tab on the dashboard (see figure 13.2 on p. 160) contains interesting reports that break down the characteristics of your visitors, right down to the types of web browsers and operating systems they use. It's probably not much use to the smaller business, but you can waste hours speculating on who is visiting you using the Opera web browser on a Linux operating system.

More useful is the *Traffic sources* page, which analyses the websites and geographic areas where your visitors come from. It can tell you how successful various campaigns are and who is referring traffic to your site.

Figure 13.1: Google Analytics

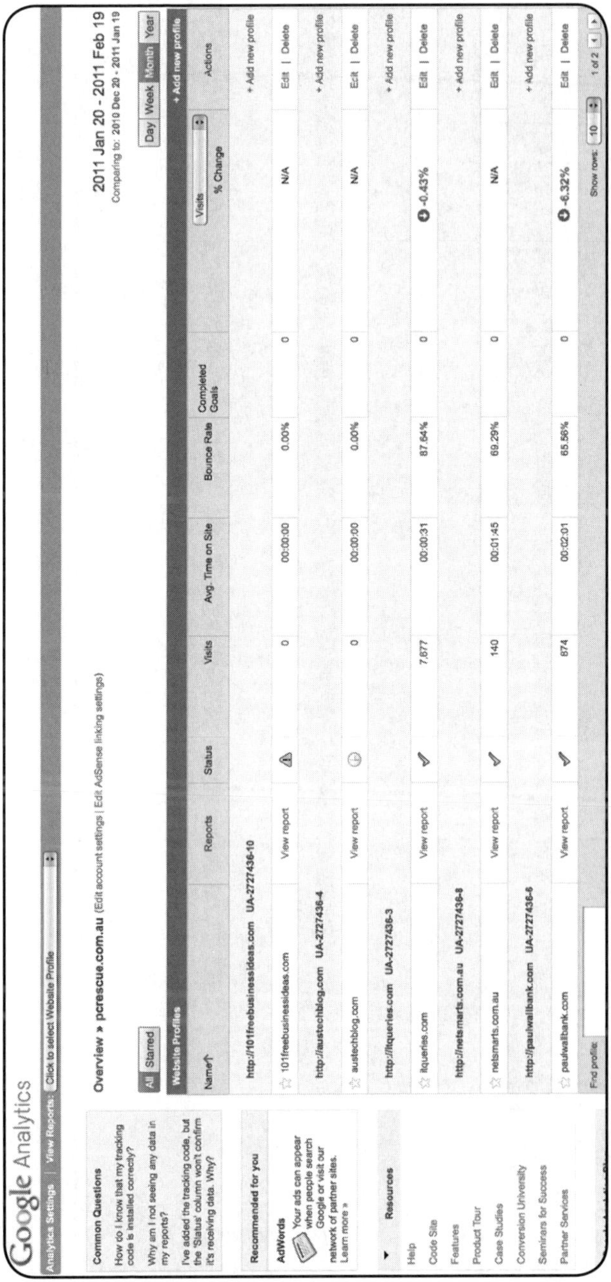

eBu$iness

Figure 13.2: Google Analytics dashboard

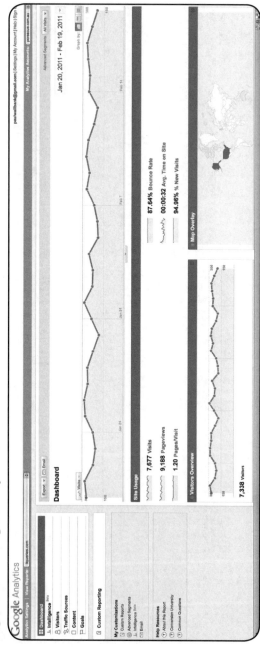

Content is very important as it tells you what visitors are reading. Along with giving the details for individual pages, it tells you where visitors came from and where they went after leaving the page.

The final tab in Google Analytics is the 'Goals' function, which allows the webmaster to set up targets for the website. For instance, if you want to funnel traffic to your sales pages or particular parts of your site, you can use the 'Goals' services to track how customers get to that page. This is very useful if you're experimenting with layouts or testing ways to get your customers to buy more from you.

Setting up Google Analytics

Visit the Google Analytics page at <www.google.com/analytics> and enter through the 'Access Analytics' button using your Google account email and password. Figure 13.3 shows the setup. The Google account password is the same as you use to enter Gmail and any of the other Google services. If you don't have a Google account, click 'Sign up now' to create one.

Figure 13.3: Google Analytics setup

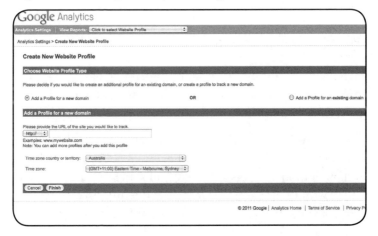

Select 'Add a new website profile' and fill in the boxes, making sure you put either http:// or https:// at the beginning of your website address, then click 'Finish'.

The next screen takes you to the script that has to be inserted into the pages on your website that you want to track. This requires some knowledge of the layout of the template or website that you are using, and you will have to copy and paste the code into the header of each page of your website.

If you're using a Wordpress site, there are some plug-ins that will do this for you. If you're using Blogger, the Analytics is built in and doesn't require anything beyond your entering the tracking code. If you are using other platforms then you may have to become familiar with editing web pages or hire a designer to do it for you.

As you or your team become more acquainted with using Google Analytics, you can use it to track specific use of pages rather than just use the same settings for the whole site.

The Google Analytics tool is a very powerful tracking tool and it's probably the most impressive freebie going on the internet; however, there are other tools you can use as well.

Hosting services

Many hosting companies have free built-in tracking tools, but most of them are based on older software, such as AWStats, one of the original free open source webmaster tools.

AWStats and the other built-in tools are adequate, but they don't have some of the advanced features of Google Analytics and other modern tools. You may find some website designers and hosting companies have a friendly, informative feature that converts AWStats's data into readable features.

Wordpress

For users of Wordpress-based sites, one useful free plug-in is the WP-Stats package (see figure 13.4), which collates visitor information to the site, and collects details from social media and other services.

Figure 13.4: Wordpress's WP-Stats

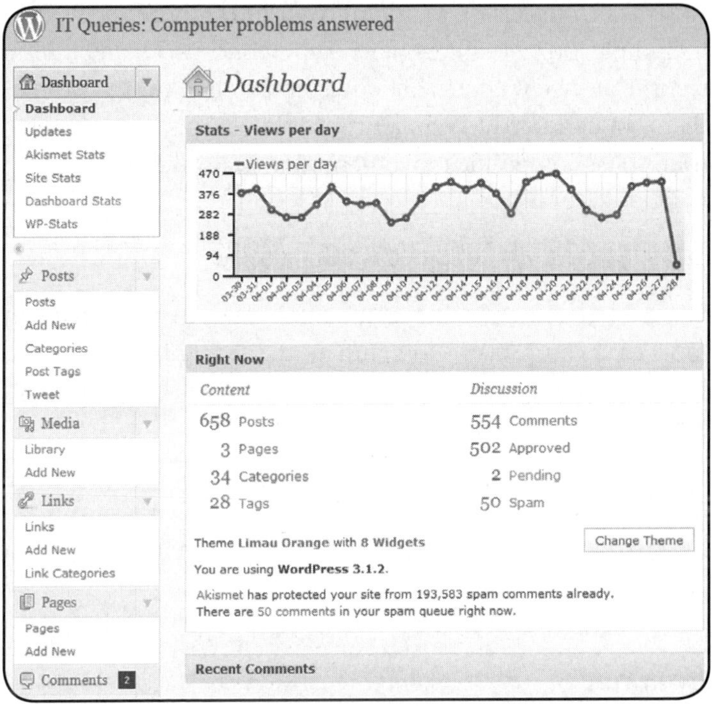

Other tracking tools

A number of commercial tracking tools are available that offer even more power than the free Google Analytics or WP-Stats. These not only pull together data from your own site and social media channels, but also analyse sentiments to gauge the negative or positive online feeling towards your brand.

The downside with these services is they can be fiendishly expensive, so they are really the playthings of big corporations and large advertising or public relations agencies. Some of these services are Alterian, Wavemetrix, Nielsen and Cymphony.

Australian businesses are doing well in this market as well, including BuzzNumbers and PeopleBrwsr. The *eBusiness* website at <www.ebusinessbook.com.au> has links to both of them. In early 2011, PeopleBrwsr was offering a 30-day free trial, so it's a good idea to look out for deals like this.

Comparing with other sites

Some of the monitoring companies offer free comparison tools that you can use to compare the traffic from your site with your competitors' as well as spy on what the big boys are doing.

Most of these comparison tools are limited in what they report—they keep the detailed reports for their paid-for versions—but they are useful for learning what the rest of the market is doing.

Compete

The free service of Compete (see figure 13.5) allows you to track the performance of up to five different sites over one year, though the premium product allows monitoring over longer time spans. The site also lists a number of key search terms that the sites attract, which is useful if you're looking at what customers are searching for when they go to the sites of your bigger competitors.

Figure 13.5: Compete comparison screen

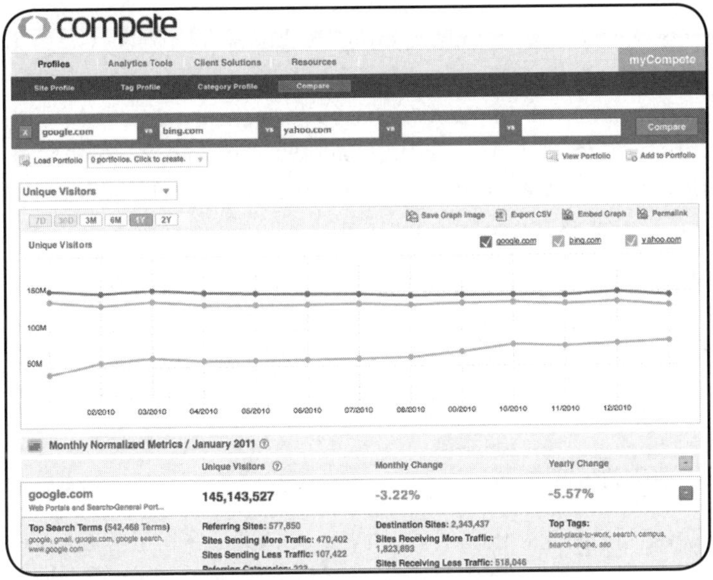

Alexa

Using a special toolbar that many web professionals install, Alexa tracks the performance of sites across the Net. Their free service allows you to view daily traffic, search engine and keyword results. For a fee, you can also see the demographics of your site's audience, such as the number of viewers aged 16–34.

Google Trends

Another of Google's free tools is their Google Trends site. While it carries out similar functions to Alexa and Compete, the data on Google Trends is far more spartan and the service tends to ignore smaller sites. In general, the other two have a far better service for tracking what your competitors are doing.

Google Website Optimizer

One of Google's interesting webmaster tools is their Website Optimizer, which allows a web designer to test the performance of different tricks and designs on a website. This function, called A/B Testing, allows the website owner or designer to insert different codes into various layouts to see what attracts the most attention.

While that's something most business owners probably won't have time to do themselves, it's worthwhile remembering this function is available, so you can ask a designer or friendly 15-year-old to test various site layouts that you are considering.

Conclusion

A/B Testing, like the other services discussed in this chapter, shows that the web is one place we don't have to worry about making guesses in business. The analytics programs show us what customers are doing on our sites, the comparison services allow us to see what our competitors are doing and the testing sites help us discover what the market wants from us.

Overall, it's a lot easier to understand what happens on the web than in many of the other areas of our business, so there's no excuse not to keep a close eye on what works.

With your website set up and designed, payment processes in place, and an eye on your customers' behaviour, it's time to look at how to attract customers to your site, and what works and what doesn't. This is the subject of step 5.

Checklist

➤ Have you signed up for a free Google Analytics account?

➤ Are you keeping track of how your site's traffic is trending?

➤ Are Google Analytics set up on all of your websites and pages?

➤ Does your site or hosting company offer other tracking tools?

➤ Are you regularly using Compete in order to compare your site's performance with others'?

➤ Do you check what keywords are popular for your biggest competitors' sites?

➤ Is your designer using A/B Testing on your site?

Step 5

Getting your name out

Chapter 14

Search engine optimisation

With your website up and running, how will you attract visitors to your site? The web is a crowded, sprawling place and standing out from the crowd is difficult for a small business. To make it worse, most customers use the major search engines to find what they want, so your business has to play by the search engines' rules to appear in a result list.

Because of the dominance of search engines, keywords have become the critical consideration for a website wanting to be found. Keywords have to reflect what your business offers and what the customers you want are looking for—so don't emphasise the word cheap if you want to attract good quality customers.

Search engines also like links to and from other websites, so the more you can add to your pages, the higher your website will be ranked in the results for a particular query. Making sure the rest of your local business community is linking to you is also useful.

Obsessing about where your pages rank on websites is pointless as the internet is a long-term thing and minor tweaks can actually damage your brand. The obsession with search engine optimisation (SEO) also distracts a site owner from other online tools, such as social media, and from putting up content that is relevant and interesting to visitors.

Who is your market?

Defining who you actually want to come to your site is an important consideration: if you're a lumber yard in Mount Gambier, you won't be too worried if people looking for hairdressing supplies in Launceston or seeking the latest TV star gossip never find you, so there's no point in trying to attract the world to your virtual door.

What exactly your market is looking for is another matter. In the case of the lumber yard, visitors are probably looking for what timber they stock, their opening hours and a contact number. Given that most local customers already know the name of the yard, it's going to be important for your website to be found under your name and location.

Where your clients are is important as well. While most people are searching on the Net using search engines, many use specific websites, social media services and forums to find products and services. Asking your customers where they found you is an important way of discovering where to focus your best online efforts.

Finding keywords

As the web is driven by the words people look for, it's worthwhile finding out exactly what words your customers are using in a search. Assuming what words customers will use to look for your products is dangerous, so don't do it.

One of the best, and free, tools to find keywords is the Google Adwords Keyword tool <https://adwords.google.com/select/KeywordToolExternal>, which is part of Google's advertising program. The Keyword tool (see figure 14.1, overleaf) allows you to type in words related to your business and see which are the most popular words used in searches.

A very useful way to find the keywords that work is to explore what words your competitors are using on their websites. Comparison sites like Alexa and Compete (see step 4) can tell you what people are searching for when they visit your competitors. It's worthwhile noting those words and seeing what the Google tool tells you about them.

As always, your customers are also a great resource: ask them how they found you and, if it was through the web, what they were looking for. You might be surprised at some of the results.

Relevant content

The obsession with optimising web pages for search engines often means website owners forget it is human beings — our customers, staff and business partners — who are the reason a business goes to the effort of setting up online.

People aren't visiting our sites because the pages have terrific SEO or can tickle a search engine's algorithms; visitors are there because they want to find out about our business, our products and how they can buy them. Our content needs to be relevant to those needs.

Figure 14.1: Google Adwords Keyword tool

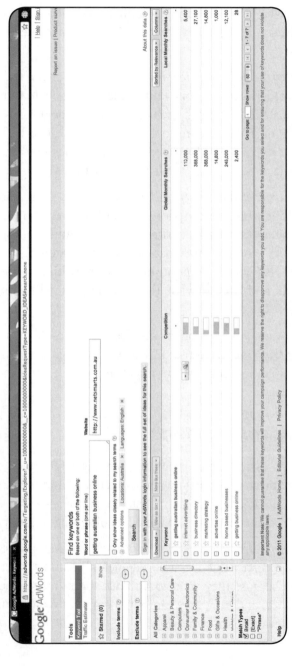

174

Sites also need to be up to date, which means adding something, at least fortnightly, that's interesting and relevant to the business or the industry your business is in. Including content that covers broader industry or consumer topics is one good way of attracting a wider readership and establishing you and your business as a leader in the field. In the case of the lumber yard, that might be occasional articles on the right type of wood for various uses or the virtues of different fasteners. For a hairdresser, it might be a regular feature on popular styles, treatments or colours. Remember, your customers are coming to you for your expertise, so show them that you and your staff *are* experts.

One area to avoid is using the business's site as a personal soapbox. If the owner of the business, or one of the employees, has strong views on potentially divisive topics such as politics, they should set up personal websites to push their views and not mix them with the business. Upsetting customers over things that are irrelevant to the day-to-day income of the enterprise is just plain silly.

Organic search

The term organic search is about meeting search engine criteria, primarily Google's, in your business area to find yourself on the first page of any search for your business.

In most competitive business sectors this can be difficult as many competitors are fighting for that elusive front page, so it's important to make sure your website includes the words your customers might look for on the web. This is called search engine optimisation (SEO).

While SEO is important, keeping your website up to date is even more vital, as other people referring to your site will attract the attention of the search engines and improve your rankings. Focusing on the basics is the best solution for long-term online success.

Search engine optimisation

There's an ongoing battle on the internet between the search engines and the SEO industry, as members of the latter try to increase their clients' ranking, while the companies such as Google and Yahoo! want to deliver interesting, relevant content to their users.

Given the search engine's key role in how web-surfers use the Net, it isn't surprising there's an obsession with how sites appear to the search engine spiders—the software used to gather information on sites.

The search engines want to deliver results that are relevant to their users: if a search produces too much pointless information, people will look elsewhere on the internet to find what they want. So the search engines have formulas, known as algorithms, to deliver correct, useful results.

SEO depends upon understanding how the search engine algorithms work and getting the highest result on the page—naturally some people try to cheat the system, which is called black hat SEO. If you use these techniques—such as cloaking, which involves creating an unreadable page designed just for search engines that redirects humans to a useful page—the search engine companies may penalise your website by taking it out of the results they display.

The lesson is not to cheat but to make sure the basic details of your business are included in your domain name and website and in all the other online channels you use, as the search engines look at social media, directories and other platforms for incoming links that confirm you are a legitimate business.

Hints for search engine success

You can do a number of basic things to ensure your site comes up well in search engine results:

→ Make sure your domain is close to your real business name.

→ Make sure the front page of your website clearly identifies what your business does and the area it serves.

→ Use keywords in your text but don't overdo them.

→ Understand the terms the public are searching for when they look for your service or product.

→ Ensure the metadata—the hidden information that describes your site to other sites—explains exactly who you are, what you do and where you do it.

→ Keep the site up to date, adding or changing some relevant information every few weeks.

→ Ensure the names and titles of individual pages reflect the contents.

→ Make sure you have links to other useful sites.

→ Use social media to keep your customers, staff and anyone else who is interested in updates informed about your business.

→ Put relevant photos, videos and documents on your website with clear, descriptive titles and reference information that explains what you do.

Paid SEO

Because SEO is so complex, a whole industry has been established around making websites friendly to search engines so that your pages come towards the top of any relevant search.

Good SEO services involve skills, patience and an under-standing of the business. A competent consultant will spend a lot of time analysing your business, markets and customers, so it's an expensive business.

As part of a business marketing plan, SEO can be very useful but a good, professional service is expensive and the results can take time. Sadly most of the market is made up of amateurs and those who are less than trustworthy.

SEO snake oil

SEO has been one of the big topics for online businesses for several years and it has given rise to a large industry. Sadly much of the advice is snake oil, offering little value beyond lining a consultant's pocket.

If the tips and tricks seem too simple and the promised results too good to be true, then they probably are. Here's some of the poor advice you might encounter.

Guaranteed number one spot

Any SEO consultant who makes that guarantee, parti-cularly on the basis of buying a particular service or software package, is kidding you. Number one spots take time and care if you are in a competitive market, and if you are not in a competitive market the number one spot doesn't matter.

Hidden links

Because search engines count outgoing links as an indication of a site's credibility, some poor advice recommends you put links to other sites on your website in such a way that only search engines can see them. If a search engine catches you doing this, you will be penalised, with your site possibly being removed from the listings altogether.

Overuse of link exchanges

Linking to other sites is important, but connecting to irrelevant sites might actually decrease your rankings. Again, if you're caught, your site will be penalised by the search engines as happened to US department store JC Penney in early 2011, when the company was caught using link exchanges, where hundreds of irrelevant sites were paid to put up references to Penney's pages.

Stuffing keywords

Keyword stuffing involves putting all the words you would like your site to be found under in your website's text. While it might make your site attractive to search engines, the text becomes unreadable for your customers.

Deceptive keywords

Unrelated keywords are a tactic to try to draw traffic to a site. Even if this does work and you get a high spot in search results, it's pointless, because the people who visit your site aren't interested in your business and have landed there by mistake.

Submitting to countless directories

Directory submission sites charge a webmaster to submit your site to dozens, sometimes hundreds, of directories. Don't bother as most of the directories are worthless.

Redesign your site

There's no doubt that some older websites aren't friendly to search engines, particularly those designed before Google became dominant. Nonetheless, a suggestion to redesign your site should be treated with caution and you should get a second opinion before following this advice.

These tricks are some of the warning signs that an SEO consultant might be one of the sharks. There are bound to be more tricks appearing, though, as SEO is a fast-evolving field.

Images and media

One of the things search engines love is media content; they reward sites that use images and video. But they have a problem in that their spiders only read text and struggle when confronted with graphics.

To overcome this, websites include a whole bunch of metadata (see figure 14.2) — information that's hidden from users but helps other computers and search engine spiders identify the content and relevance of the image.

Figure 14.2: webpage metadata

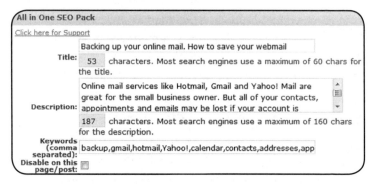

Yahoo! has some useful guidelines for webmasters about this, and you will find a link to the site on the *eBusiness* website at <www.ebusinessbook.com.au>. The advice includes the following.

Name

The name of a media file or link is critical. For instance, if the lumber yard website showed some timber decking, naming the associated images would be along the lines of 'spotted_gum_decking_joes_lumber_yard.jpg'. Note the use of underlining to space the words, as spaces don't work well for internet file names.

Title

Not to be confused with the actual file's name or caption, the title is given to the file by the business owner, designer or webmaster and is embedded in the site. Again, the title should be descriptive and there's no reason the title can't be the same as the file's name.

Alternative text

'Alt' tags are important on all websites as they are used by accessibility programs to identify what the link or file is about. A brief explanation of the link or media file has the happy result of both improving the search engine results for your site and helping sight-impaired users navigate it easily.

Caption

The caption is exactly that: the wording that goes with the document or file and describes or names what is shown in the image. Be careful of this attribute, because many site templates will put the caption text underneath the image, which can mess up the design of some sites.

Description

Go mad! This attribute allows you to pile on the superlatives and really get into detail. Every keyword you have identified that is suitable for your site or products should be included in this box as this will give the search engines opportunities to index more relevant information on your page.

Image size

While it isn't a search engine issue, it's also important to consider the size of the images you install, as big image files can slow your site down and make it less user friendly. Try to keep images below 100 kb and don't overload sites with unnecessary pictures.

Local search

The location-based services discussed in step 1 are a critical part of being found on the web for most businesses, as most sell to the local population. Also, the keywords in local listings feed into the search engines. Given that most customers are looking for local businesses, having a presence in the local search directories is probably more important for most organisations. Getting the local listing right is the most important thing for most small businesses.

For Australian businesses, the two main local directories are Google Places and True Local. Both are free and each has certain advantages (see step 1), but both services love detail, and the more detail you can give about your service and products, the higher your listing will be when locals start looking for you using the search engines.

The content on the local search platforms adds to your website's credibility in the search engine rankings, so good, relevant content in local descriptions will improve your site's performance on the wider search engines.

Offline channels

Don't underestimate the offline world for driving traffic to your website. People see the signage on your car and business, along with any advertising and sponsorships you do. All your offline marketing, public relations and advertising should point back to your website by including your web address.

Conclusion

Getting noticed on the web is an increasingly important part of being in business, but it's best to do it with good, long-term thinking and valuable consumer content. Don't go for quick runs with dubious search engine marketing.

While providing sound, up-to-date information that considers how the search engines work can drive customers to your website and your business, you will also want to consider how paid advertising online can help your business grow. That's the subject of chapter 15.

Checklist

➤ Have you listed on the local search platforms described in step 1?

➤ Do you know which keywords your customers are using?

➤ Have you ensured your site's description is consistent with the local search listings discussed in step 1?

➤ Have you ensured the keywords essential for your business are included in the metadata and content on your site?

➤ Have you made sure you have detailed product descriptions on your website?

➤ Does all your marketing material, from your business card to the name on your van, include your website address?

➤ Are all the images and links on your site properly described in their metadata?

Chapter 15
Paid advertising

Despite all the clever things you can do on your website to attract visitors, it is still worth using paid advertisements to spread the word about your business—and the good news is that online advertising is far easier and much cheaper than the offline alternatives.

Small business advertising has been the cash cow of the publishing industry for two centuries—a well-thought-out advertisement in a newspaper, phone directory or magazine has often been the first step in establishing the foundation of a commercial empire. At the very least, the local classifieds and Yellow Pages have been the main way smaller businesses have traditionally advertised.

Today advertising is moving online as readers and, more importantly, customers turn to the web for news and entertainment. What makes online channels great for small business is that campaigns are cheaper, easier to set up and far more measurable for establishing their impact than a print or broadcast commercial. For small business another plus is that most online advertising doesn't require the upfront costs expected in other media, and it is usually charged on a pay per click basis, which means you pay only for the customers who click on your ad. It means you can launch an online ad campaign for as little as $50.

You can use a number of competing networks and social media channels for advertising, including social media, such as LinkedIn and Facebook, along with the major web advertisers, such as Google.

One of the great advantages of online advertising is that advertising websites are largely self-service, so you don't have to deal with an aggressive sales force trying to upsell you to a more expensive program or a call centre, where you're sure the operator will get your details wrong. Most importantly, you preview things before publishing.

If you decide midway through the campaign that things aren't working, it is easy to change or even cancel the advertisement. This aspect alone makes online advertising more attractive to agile and quick-moving small and new businesses.

CPC and CPM

When you are advertising online, two important terms will jump out at you, CPC and CPM. These terms refer to two of the ways online ads are measured and paid for.

CPM stands for clicks per mille, the mille being Latin for thousand, which is the advertising industry trying to impress us with their expensive educations. CPM is the traditional way of measuring mass advertising based on the ratings of TV shows or newspaper sales. Advertising on a CPM arrangement means you will be charged by each thousand page views.

CPC, or cost per click, is the more advanced way of measuring online advertising: you pay only for the actual clicks on your advertisement. This adds a great deal more accountability to campaigns and allows you to directly track costs and effectiveness of both individual ads and platforms.

Of the two choices, it's usually best to choose the CPC option, which is generally more effective. The CPM model can work, but it's usually used for larger, broader campaigns, which are generally beyond the budget of smaller businesses.

A handy monitoring tactic with online advertising is to create a landing page—a specially created page for your marketing campaign that will allow you to track exactly how effective the program has been. A landing page will elaborate on the offer in the advertisement and should drive customers to purchasing the product. Properly monitored, a landing page can be a really useful tool to measure return on investment.

Google Adwords

The most valuable advertising platform in the world today is Google: of the US$29 billion the company earned in 2010, US$28 billion came from online advertisements, and the bulk of that came from Adwords. Keyword advertising on the Net is a very lucrative business.

While it's profitable for Google, Adwords is also very useful for advertisers, not only being cheaper than traditional classified and display advertising, but also being more targeted. Google's Adwords service looks at the website and chooses an advertisement related to the content. This makes

Adwords a very focused method of advertising—only searchers looking for that word will see the ads.

To use Google Adwords, just visit the Adwords site at <www.google.com.au/adwords> and sign up (see figure 15.1). This is simple, and if you already have a Google account for one of their other services it's straightforward.

Figure 15.1: Google Adwords signup page

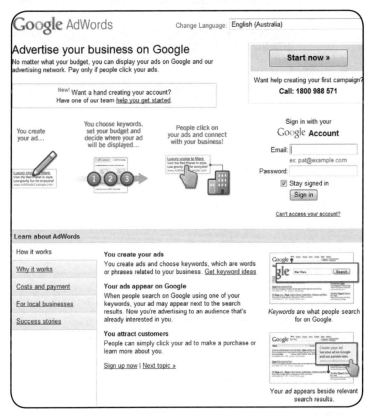

A few minutes later you should receive an email to confirm your signup, and with that email you can get on with setting up your first online Google Adwords campaign.

The first Adwords screen will ask you about your geographic location (see figure 15.2). You can choose from one of the suggested locations, which usually are worldwide, country, state or city, with an option of adding other locations as well. Unless you're selling to the entire world, it's best to restrict your location to the area you operate in.

Figure 15.2: Google Adwords campaign setup

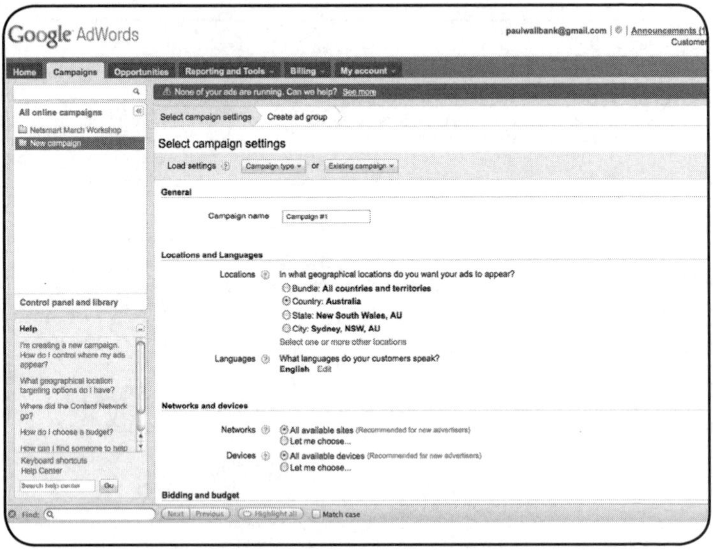

Fill in the CPC (cost per click) you're comfortable with. Keep in mind if you are bidding on a popular keyword your ad won't be seen unless you bid high. If you bid too high, you might blow your budget. A typical choice for starters is $1 CPC, with a limit of $25 a day, but you can go right down to one cent or put in bids for tens of thousands of dollars per click.

Google also may vary the minimum bid amount. While most words in the bid will be one cent, popular words can creep up in price and have been known to get as high as $10 per click.

Like many things with Google, their formula for determining a minimum bid is cloaked in secrecy.

In the Ad Extensions, below the cost, you can choose to associate the ad with your Google Places account, which is a good idea. The other options give you the opportunity to connect your ad with your phone number, which is useful for people who find you on their mobile, and to add links to your site.

When you're finished, click 'Save and continue' to go onto the next page where you can design your ad (see figure 15.3).

Figure 15.3: setting up a Google Adwords advertisement

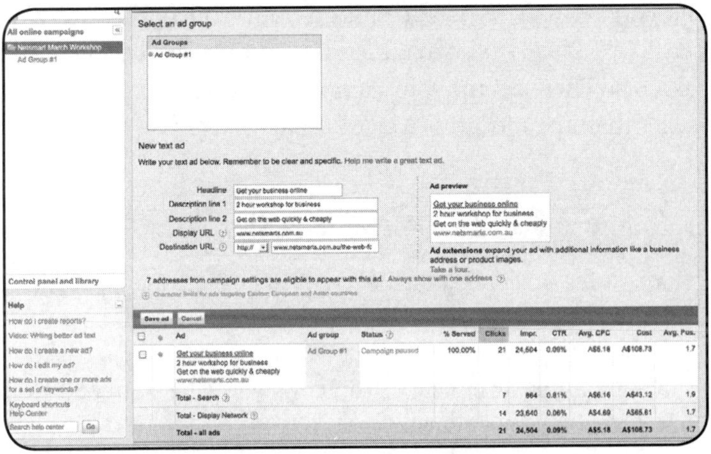

In the 'Create ads and keywords' section you will write your advertisement and choose the web page it will link to. In the keywords section, Google will suggest words and phrases: you don't have to accept them but, if you do, make sure you add some of the keywords you discovered for your business when you worked through step 5.

Click on 'Estimate search summary' and you will get an estimate of the clicks and costs Google thinks you will receive with the combination of keywords you have chosen. Note that this is an estimate and not a guarantee: if you're unlucky you may find you end up pay nothing, as no-one clicks them.

In the next screen you're asked to confirm your country and you will then move on to the payments section. Fill in the 'Usual payments' section, noting the difference between the pre-paid options, which allow you to limit payments by posting a deposit up front, and the post-paid options, which can expose you to higher bills.

If you have received one of Google's free trial vouchers (see the box on special offers), this is the time to use it. Enter the code *exactly* as it appears on your voucher, as it's case sensitive, usually all capital letters, and you will redeem the voucher. That sets up your campaign. Altogether this is a lot easier than the old print way of doing things.

Google Adwords special offers

One of the interesting things about Google as a company is its obsession with discount vouchers, and much of its own marketing to small business is through giving out vouchers offering a free advertising trial worth anywhere from $50 to $100 to attract customers.

It's worthwhile checking before signing up if you are eligible for any of these offers. You may find that your hosting company, professional organisation or local chamber of commerce also has an offer for customers and members.

If you use a discount or free trial offer, make sure that you define the limits on your advertising campaign or else you may find your $75 discount covers only a tiny fraction of the total bill.

Other online advertising services

Like most things on the web, Google may be the biggest game in town, but it certainly isn't the only advertising platform. A host of smaller services may be useful channels for some businesses.

Yahoo! and Microsoft

To counter the Google monolith, Microsoft has joined their Bing advertising service with Yahoo! In theory, the two of them together should be a potent competitor for Google, but the service isn't available in Australia, so it's irrelevant to this book at the moment.

Chitika and Adbrite

Two other competitors in the online advertising space are Chitika and Adbrite. Both offer some advantages over Google, such as better advertisements and payments in some niche industries, but generally their performance isn't as good. Chitika was responsible for a wave of ugly weight reduction ads that infested the internet in 2009 and 2010.

Social media advertising

One of the big changes in the online world in recent years has been the growth of social media sites such as LinkedIn and Facebook. As most social media services don't charge their users for access, one of their main sources of revenue is advertising.

Social media advertising has a number of advantages over other channels, particularly given that the services know a lot more about their users than other service providers, so it's possible to target ads to very specific individuals and groups. This can make placing ads on a social network attractive to many businesses.

Keep in mind when considering social media that there are a lot of myths about who uses these services, with the assumption being that kids are the main users of them. In reality, people of all ages are using social media services, with grandparents currently being the fastest growing group on Facebook.

Facebook

With more than 500 million users, Facebook is the most obvious place to advertise on the web. It also has the advantage of having an extremely clean and simple interface, making it easy to create an ad.

Starting the Facebook advertising setup is very easy. Log on then go to <www.facebook.com/advertising>. The page will give you an overview of how the service works and some successful case studies. It's worthwhile reading these to get some idea of the terminology.

When you're ready to start, click on the green 'create an ad' button and the *What do you want to advertise* screen appears. At the very top you'll have the option of choosing the page to associate with the campaign. You can choose your business or events page that we discussed in chapter 3.

You get a choice of sponsored stories, which appear in the news or wall feed, or ads, which appear to the right of screen. Generally ads are better if you're trying to reach new customers.

The wording of your advert is very important so make sure you include the key words that will attract the right customers to your site. An eye-catching image always helps as well.

Because Facebook tries to collect comprehensive data, it allows you to zone in on particular suburbs and the surrounding areas, advertise to people on their birthdays and other important dates, and differentiate your advertising by the audience's interests and occupations.

As you choose your advertising options, Facebook will update exactly how many people you will reach in your target audience and suggest how much your individual clicks will cost. You can change the maximum bid, but it's best to leave it to Facebook until you're experienced enough to know what works.

When narrowing your options don't be too conservative. It is tempting to think you can target your audience precisely and save some money at the same time but it's far more likely you'll miss key targets. For instance, if you're selling perfume you'll miss much of the gift trade by choosing to exclude males from your advertising.

Don't stress too much about getting it right first time as you can change the ad and test the various responses to different words and selections while it's running.

One really good feature of Facebook is that you can specify the times the ad appears. Choosing the time slot when your customers are most likely to be on the web maximises the opportunities for the right people to see your ad.

Click through to the payment screen and you will be given the choice of paying by PayPal or credit card. Complete the process, enter any codes for discount vouchers you may have received, and Facebook will ask you to log in again and confirm your details. The ad campaign will then start.

Once the ad starts, Facebook will email you daily on the progress of your ad, including sales to date, changes to accounts and, most importantly, if Facebook chooses not to approve your advertisement because they think it is outside their terms of service.

LinkedIn advertising

If your target market is business professionals, particularly in the tech, sales and human resources fields, LinkedIn is an excellent resource and, like Facebook, it has the advantage of being narrowly targeted.

To start advertising, you have to find the well-hidden link labelled 'Advertising' at the bottom of the screen and follow the prompts. From there, you will follow a similar process to setting up your advertising on Adwords and Facebook (see figure 15.4).

Figure 15.4: LinkedIn configuration page

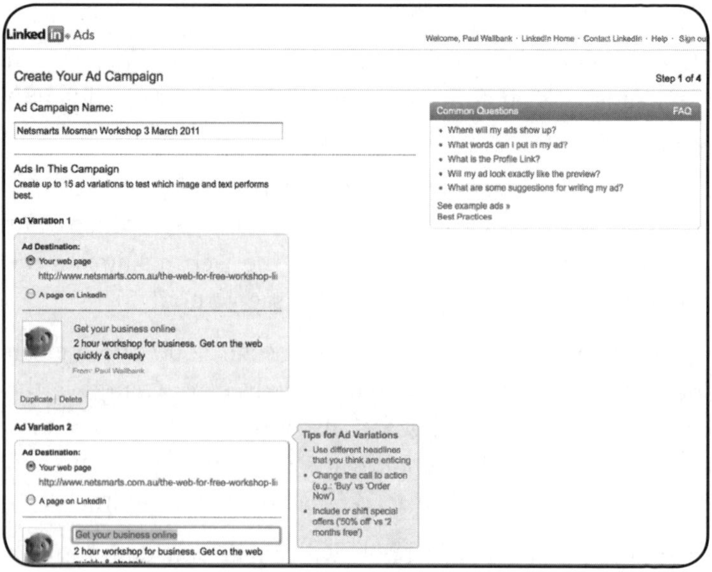

One of the great things about LinkedIn advertising is that you can test up to 15 different advertising layouts to see which works best in practice. If you're new to online advertising, it's worthwhile using this feature to experiment, although because of LinkedIn's professional user base, any lessons learnt won't translate perfectly across to the broader Adwords and Facebook platforms.

On the *Targeting* page (see figure 15.5), LinkedIn will ask you to narrow down your selections. If you don't use this feature, the advertisement will automatically go worldwide to everyone. Like Facebook, LinkedIn will show you your potential audience size as you select various demographics.

Figure 15.5: LinkedIn targeting page

The payment page will ask the usual questions for a credit card payment—unlike Facebook, LinkedIn doesn't accept PayPal—and you will also have the opportunity to add the details of any discount coupon you have received.

Once your LinkedIn campaign is running you will be able to monitor its progress through the *Reporting* page (see figure 15.6, overleaf), which will tell you how much you have spent to date and the number of clicks and impressions the ad has received.

Figure 15.6: LinkedIn reporting page

Conclusion

Online advertising is one of the best things the internet has given small business. It has increased choice, accountability and affordability for advertisers. The ease of placing and monitoring online advertising campaigns makes the Net the best platform for running marketing campaigns.

Each of the advertising platforms—Google Adwords, Facebook and LinkedIn—brings its own benefits and advantages, and it's up to you to decide which channel works best for you. The beauty with these platforms, particularly the social media services, is you can target closely who will see your ad. Step 6 adds more detail about using the social media to promote your business, by creating fans and customers.

Checklist

> ➤ Have you developed a good list of keywords that relate to your business?

> ➤ Have you decided which channels are appropriate for your markets?

> ➤ Have you determined the budget you can afford?

> ➤ Have you crafted advertisements that target exactly the customers you want?

> ➤ Have you set up a way to measure and monitor what works for your business?

> ➤ Have you created specific landing pages for your advertisements?

> ➤ Are you prepared to change an ad that you find doesn't work?

Step 6

Creating fans and customers

Chapter 16
Social media rules

Both the organisation of your website and the use of paid advertising can bring existing and prospective customers to your website. Word of mouth can too and social media is the internet's equivalent of townsfolk gossiping in the market square.

We have always known word of mouth is the most valuable marketing tool: 200 years ago it was the only way that most businesses could get their name out to potential customers. Social media is today's electronic equivalent of the town marketplace or the village pub. People are talking about you, and your reputation is being built or trashed on it.

As well as offering a free way to get online (see step 1), social media is also an effective way to drive traffic to your website, as well as brand your business with key consumers and opinion makers.

It should be emphasised that social media tools aren't for every business: for some they aren't relevant and others simply don't have the time and resources that most social media channels demand. Although no business—or individual owners and managers—should ignore them, for those for whom social media is the right tool it is a very powerful asset to the business.

Often social media channels are dismissed as toys for bored teenagers and twenty-somethings. In reality, LinkedIn has become the online CV for professionals and an important human resources tool; Twitter is dominated by the 30–50 year age group, particularly in marketing and media; and Facebook's fastest growing user group is grandparents.

Social media rules

- Show respect to everyone. Even people you find disturbing.

- Listen to users, because once you have filtered out the crazies, you will find the collective intelligence of the web can be quite powerful.

- Conduct a conversation. The big currency in social media is conversation: by joining in with constructive comments you enhance your reputation.

- Be constructive; add value to the conversation.

- Be positive. The web rewards the positive more than the negative: by all means post critical comments, but it's best for your posts to be more positive than negative.

- Be honest. Social media has a horrible way of catching people out, so don't tell lies.

- Associate with the smart kids. You're judged by the company you keep, just like in the school playground.

- Don't constantly plug your services. You will be branded a spammer and shunned.

- Social media is not a numbers game. Don't obsess about the number of Twitter followers or Facebook friends you have. Quality beats quantity every time.

- Never post when you are drunk or feeling emotional. You will regret it.

- Step away. If you find a social media channel is taking up too much of your time or passion, take a break.

- Use what you've learned.

Social media's attractions are that it is more than just a marketing tool. For many, it works for gathering industry intelligence, providing customer service, catching up on the news and developing new networks. For most users, social media is something they use to enhance both their personal and business lives.

Watching the feeds

One important business application for social media, particularly Twitter and Facebook, is monitoring what your customers are saying about you. For this reason it's worthwhile logging on at least once a day, just to check what people have said about you in the major channels.

If someone is complaining, it's an opportunity to publicly engage with them and show them that you care about fixing their problems — often just showing you're a real person who empathises with their issues can turn the harshest critic into a great supporter.

Fans shouldn't be ignored either: if someone compliments you online, it is worthwhile to reward them with a small gift or freebie. This can turn a happy customer into a raving fan.

Don't delete the bad stuff

A key rule in social media is not to delete critical posts. It's far better to leave them on the wall or forum and engage with the critic. If the unhappy customer turns nasty, disengage with them and leave their aggressive comments standing.

Where you should delete inappropriate posts is when they are offensive, defamatory or likely to incite illegal acts. Many people have the strange idea that the physical world's laws don't apply online—they do and if you can be shown to have permitted illegal or damaging online comments then you might be held liable.

You should also watch your own behaviour, as various aspects of consumer protection rules, and corporations and trade practices laws are particularly appropriate to online forums. Engaging in misleading conduct about your, or your competitors', products is a quick way to find yourself falling foul of the law.

There is no shortage of social media channels—everything from the mainstream Facebook through to niche services like DeviantArt, a site for artists and creatives, and forums that discuss specific topics, ranging from broadband networks to scrapbooking and trainspotting. We'll look at a few of the major channels.

Twitter

Based upon mobile phone text messages, Twitter is a powerful tool for marketing, but the micro-messaging platform is more about listening, learning and having conversations with your customers, staff, suppliers and industry.

The key to success on Twitter is who you follow—your Twitter screen will fill up with the latest tweets from those you follow—so choosing the right people will avoid the 'what I had for breakfast' crowd and get you value and in turn add worth to your followers.

After setting up a Twitter account (see step 1), a list of interests appears. Choosing various areas that interest you leads you to a page that suggests people you should follow. Anybody you think is interesting can be followed by clicking on the 'Follow' link. Their tweets will then appear on your Twitter page.

It's usually best to start by following a few people and watching what they say and do over a few days. You will find people start following you on the strength of your profile and followers, this happens even if you never send a tweet yourself.

Posting tweets

It's not a good idea to blast your Twitter followers with promotions for your products. People who do that don't really get any value from Twitter, as the medium rewards conversations rather than advertisements.

You can trigger conversations with customers and others in your industry by posting tweets containing links to worthy and relevant articles. As you do this, you will start to pick up followers who are interested in your industry, and hopefully your business, which in turn drives traffic to your website, where you have a chance to convert them to customers.

As you get into Twitter conversations with your customers, you will find they start referring links and retweeting—that is repeating—your posts, which will build your followers and in turn your credibility.

The biggest limitation for Twitter is the 140-character limit to each post. So it isn't the medium for long essays. The limit also means it's difficult to post many web links, as it's common for a web address on its own to be well over the 140 character maximum. To overcome this, there are URL shortening tools such as <www.bit.ly> that reduce the size of the link.

Keeping track of conversations can be hard and the Twitter website isn't always the easiest way to do it. Desktop software, such as Hootsuite and Tweetdeck, make management easier and have useful features built in, such as automatic link shortening.

LinkedIn

If your business caters to professionals or you're in the human resources and recruitment industries, LinkedIn is one of the most useful tools for growing your business.

LinkedIn can basically be described as having an online CV, where colleagues and potential employers can check out your experience and qualifications. However, features such as discussion groups can grow your business's credibility.

Joining or setting up a group (see figure 16.1) is extremely easy, although many professional groups now require approval of new members to prevent rogue recruitment agents joining and bothering everybody.

Participating in a group is a great way of establishing your credibility with people in the same field as you. This is really useful if you're a consultant or professional who needs to show your expertise and knowledge.

The update function, where you post what you are currently doing, is a useful tool as well, as informative updates, like those in Twitter, enhance your reputation and professional profile. You can also use the update function to link back to events and group postings you have made on LinkedIn.

Figure 16.1: LinkedIn groups

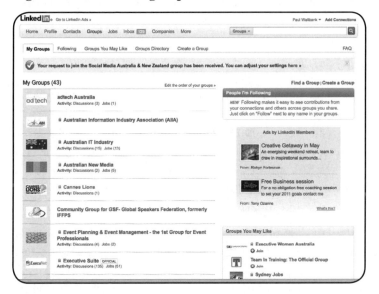

Facebook

The big bear of all social media channels is Facebook, with more than 500 million users doing things ranging from liking and commenting on each other's posts through to playing online games and buying virtual goods.

Most businesses engage with Facebook users through the organisation's Facebook page (see step 1). Individuals can also set up their own fan or hate pages about a business as well.

As with the other social media, it's important to engage with users regardless of what they say about you. Quite a few large brands, such as Nestlé, have made the mistake of deleting or attempting to shut down critical points of view, which only makes the problem worse.

One of the best ways to promote your business is to get people to 'like' your business, posts or products, as this then puts your product on their wall. Posting news and details about new products on Facebook is a good way to improve the coverage of your business.

Forums

One of the older, but still powerful, ways to build a following is through the use of forums. Forums are websites where users can make comments, post ideas and generally have conversations about the topics at hand. Forums are also a great way to connect with the opinion leaders in your industry. You will find some of the participants have deep knowledge, experience and contacts, which can help your business as well.

There are forums for almost every conceivable topic, from video games to horse floats, and all of the regular posters in them are passionate about their particular interest. That passion makes forums a very powerful way of engaging customers and the industry.

If you are hosting your own website, it's possible to set up your own forum, but this exposes your business to risks, such as users posting illegal or defamatory comments, which your organisation, and possibly you personally, could be held responsible for. Generally the resources required to control a forum are beyond those of a small business. But in most cases, setting up your own forum isn't necessary, as there are already dozens that will probably cover your industry. When you sign up to someone's forum, just remember it is their property and their rules apply, so respect their rules and conventions.

Generally, when you sign up to a forum, or any other social media service, as a business it's best to use the organisation's name, so it is clear who you are and what you represent.

Some forums will allow you to have a link to your website in your profile, but almost all will frown on, if not be actively hostile to, shameless plugging of your service, so don't do it.

Other social media services

Hundreds of social platforms are available on the Net (see step 1), but we won't go into detail about them here, as even the biggest book couldn't cover this huge and rapidly changing field.

Conclusion

For businesses, the main attraction of the various social media platforms is that they are great for building a brand and reputation with customers, employees and suppliers. Done properly, using social media can be a great way to spread the word about how good you are at what you do.

Checklist

> Have you chosen the services that are relevant to your customers and staff?

> Have you signed up in your business name wherever possible?

> Did you remember to include your website details and contact in your profile?

> Remember to show respect in all your posts and discussions.

> Remember not to spam.

> Always try to engage and share ideas.

> Respond to criticism, don't delete it, and reward fans.

> Don't obsess or be paranoid about critics.

Chapter 17
Staying in touch

Just as social media allows us to talk to the world, there is one specific group we need to keep in contact with—our clients. In the struggle to find new clients and respond to changing markets, we often take existing customers for granted, though our existing clients are the most valuable asset we have. Various online tools, such as email newsletters, social media and websites, make it easier than ever for us to retain our precious clientele.

How a business stays in touch with clients has evolved over the years. Once we met them in the town square or village pub; then newspapers came along and we started publishing notices—if you look at a nineteenth-century newspaper you will see the front page is plastered in advertisements and announcements; then came radio and television; and when printing became cheap, direct mail became a popular way of reaching customers.

The internet, and specifically email, has changed how we keep our customers informed. Suddenly we had easy-to-use messaging that delivered our news direct to our customers — best of all, it was almost free.

While the social media channels are catching up with email for disseminating news, and the older methods are still valid — and when used well, probably more powerful — email remains the most popular way for us to engage with our customer base today.

Email newsletters

As any spammer sending messages advertising pills or investment scams will tell you, the beauty of email is that it's almost free and very easy to send — that's why it is so popular with businesses. That's not to say it's hassle-free though: there are routing problems, false spam alerts and just the sheer fatigue many internet users experience as a result of dozens of emails a day. To use email well, you need a good tool.

MailChimp

Many email messaging programs are available — some from hosting companies and others stand alone. One of the best small business email tools is MailChimp, which is free for businesses with mailing lists of less than 2000 who send fewer than 12 000 emails a month.

It is a terrific program. It manages your mailing list; allows you to write and edit newsletters; and tracks who has opened the email and the links they have opened. It also includes some good plug-ins for the popular web platforms to make signup forms easier.

Designing email newsletters and marketing campaigns is a bit of an art—get something wrong and often people simply won't open the message. So one of MailChimp's big benefits is that it has really useful video tutorials on how to build an effective email campaign (see figure 17.1).

Figure 17.1: MailChimp screen

Source: MailChimp® is a registered trademark of The Rocket Science Group.

MailChimp's templates also help ensure compliance with the *Spam Act*, which requires that we seek the recipient's consent to email them, identify ourselves and give recipients an easy way to unsubscribe. MailChimp logs the details of a client's signup and adds clear and easy unsubscribe instructions to every email, which frees the business owner from ensuring those essential details are complied with.

To create an email campaign in MailChimp is simple: create a new account with MailChimp and once you're in the dashboard click on the 'Create campaign' button (see figure 17.2).

Once you are in the *Create campaign* screen (see figure 17.3 on p. 214), you will be asked to choose the mailing list you want to use. If you haven't already got one, this is the time to start collecting email addresses. Hopefully you will already have a healthy list of clients' email addresses.

Figure 17.2: MailChimp dashboard

Source: MailChimp® is a registered trademark of The Rocket Science Group.

Copying address books

Your contact list is probably the single most important file you have on your office computers. Backing it up and sharing it with other applications is an important factor in using mailing lists in programs such as MailChimp and customer relationship management programs. Luckily, there's a standard format that most contact lists understand called comma separated value (CSV). It saves the database into a single spreadsheet-like format and you can then export the database back into a file.

On most Windows or Mac email and contact programs you can find the export function by going to 'File' and then 'Export', which will either start a wizard or just export the file to an appropriate location. If asked, select the CSV option.

Importing a CSV file into another program such as MailChimp uses the opposite procedure, using a file import function in the contact list settings.

If you want to share a contact list between your computer and a contact application, both Windows and Mac computers have features that let you connect into services such as Gmail or Yahoo! Mail. If you want to share contacts between employees, then you will have to use services such as Highrise, the professional version of Google Apps or SalesForce.

Figure 17.3: setting up a MailChimp campaign

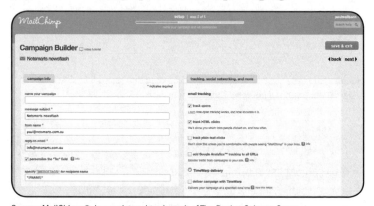

Source: MailChimp® is a registered trademark of The Rocket Science Group.

These basic questions are quite important, you need to give the campaign a unique name and generally it's a good idea to include the date in the name so you can track the campaign later. The subject line is extremely important, as a vague or boring headline won't encourage time-poor or jaded customers to open your email.

Once you have filled in the details, click 'Next' to go to the screen that lets you choose the newsletter layout. Like many of the social media and blogging tools already discussed, MailChimp has a range of ready-made, free and premium templates, as well as offering the option to design your own.

Having selected a template, enter the title, content and any side panels by clicking on each element—a completed newsletter is shown in figure 17.4. MailChimp's interface is a bit flaky here, and it's not unknown for it to lose your work if you aren't very careful. It's a good idea to create the content in your word processing program first, then copy and paste the completed newsletter into the content field.

Figure 17.4: a completed newsletter in MailChimp

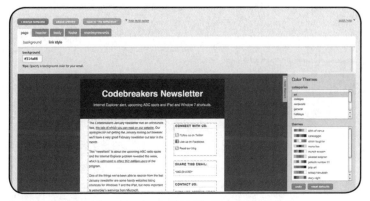

Source: MailChimp® is a registered trademark of The Rocket Science Group.

Once you're happy with all the details, click 'Next' and you can check that everything is correct before sending or scheduling the mailout for a future time. Both buttons are at the bottom of the screen.

After the message has gone, MailChimp's reporting system will start compiling the results of your campaign (see figure 17.5, overleaf). It will build reports on hard bounces (mail that can't be delivered because the email address is no longer available) and soft bounces (mail that can't be delivered because there's a temporary problem, for example the mailbox is full or out of order).

Within an hour or two, the mailing report will start to have meaningful results on your mailout. The key statistics are opens (how many people have opened the message), how many were bounced, how many were returned, how many were unopened, as well as click rate and how many messages had links in them clicked. There are also comparison statistics against your industry, so you can check how your email campaign compares with others'.

Figure 17.5: MailChimp reporting on an email campaign

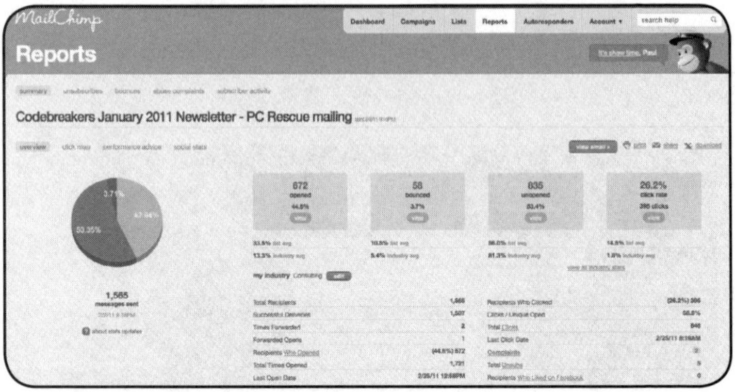

Source: MailChimp® is a registered trademark of The Rocket Science Group.

MailChimp isn't the only email management program, and it's worth having a look at what others in your industry use. It may be that you find another solution works better for you.

Surveys

One of the really useful tools for engaging with your clients is surveys. Customers really seem to like filling in basic online questionnaires and they are a great resource for your own business research. They can be used for publicity purposes or to gauge customer satisfaction with your services.

Setting up surveys is very easy. The two main free business tools are the built-in forms function in the Google Docs suite and SurveyMonkey. Both are quick and easy to set up.

SurveyMonkey

The free SurveyMonkey service offers up to 100 responses per survey and 10 surveys a month. The various professional—read paid—services, which range from $30 a month to a $1000 a year, allow more surveys and have additional features that are useful if your business is a heavy user of customer statistics and research.

For most, the free surveys are adequate and simple to set up, as shown in figure 17.6. Once you've signed up for a SurveyMonkey account, click on the 'Create survey' button. After your have given the project a name, you will be given the choice of a custom design or one of the standard templates. The standard templates are usually fine, unless you want a custom look. Note, however, that some of the standard designs are available only to SurveyMonkey Pro's customers.

Figure 17.6: SurveyMonkey startup screen

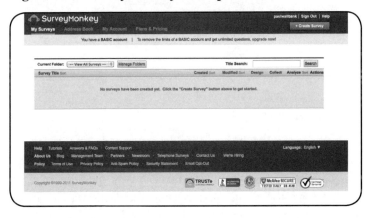

Having designed the survey or selected a template, you will get the opportunity to integrate it into emails and websites or share it on Facebook. Depending on the objectives of the survey, you may want to invite the public to respond or restrict responses to your customers.

As results come in, you can review the progress and responses in the 'Analyze results' tab (see figure 17.7) and distribute them to your staff or clients, or build them into reports suitable for press releases or external contractors.

Figure 17.7: SurveyMonkey report

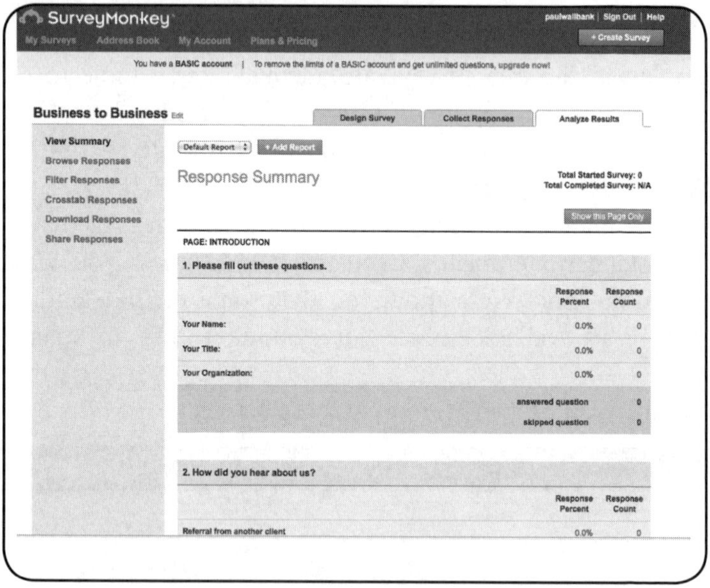

Google forms

Built into both the free and paid versions of Google's online office suite, the Google Apps forms feature is a nifty and free service that allows you to set up a survey quickly. While it doesn't have the range of templates and lacks the advanced features SurveyMonkey offers, it is free and fairly easy to set up.

To access it, you will need a Google Mail (Gmail) account (see step 4). Once in Gmail, click on the 'Documents' button at the top of the screen and you will be taken to the Google Docs view (see figure 17.8).

Figure 17.8: Google Docs screen

In the Google Docs view, click on the 'Create new' button, and a list of options drops down; for surveys, the option is 'Form'. The *Form* screen (figure 17.9) will take you through a series of windows where you can design each question for your survey. When you're ready to move on to the next question, click 'Done'— you can also choose whether to set a question as mandatory for those completing the form—and fill in the next details.

Figure 17.9: Google forms design

An interesting feature of Google forms, as shown in figure 17.9, is the types of answers you can choose—everything from a simple text choice through to sliding scales (e.g. 'rate this from 1 to 10' questions) and grid placements. This makes Google forms quite useful for more detailed questionnaires, which is an advantage over services such as SurveyMonkey.

Like all the Google Docs applications, the forms are saved as you work on them. You can see what the form looks like by clicking on 'You can view the published form here' at the bottom of the page. If you don't like how it looks, edit the questions by clicking the pencil icon to the right of each question; you can change the background by clicking on 'Theme' at the top of the page and selecting a theme from the nearly 100 available.

To view the Google forms results, click on 'See responses' at the top of the page, which will open a spreadsheet that can be manipulated into various charts and reports. It also offers the option of downloading to your own computer for saving and further editing.

Google forms is a little bit rougher than SurveyMonkey, but it does have the advantage of more advanced reporting and customisation in its free version. Both are really useful tools for any small business.

Social media

As discussed in step 6, the social media tools are a great way to develop a community. Encouraging your customers to 'like' you on Facebook and LinkedIn, while following you on Twitter, can give them early notice of special offers, while also allowing them to give you feedback.

The advantage of social media is that it's public, so others can see how you interact with your customers and how enthusiastic they are about your products. Customer engagement can actually become a marketing tool.

Similarly with Twitter, you can encourage your customers to follow you. If they like what you're doing and retweet, then you will get attention from their followers, which in turn helps to grow your online and physical business.

It's worth considering what angles you can use in social media for customer retention. As it's a new and quickly evolving field, some creative thinking can give you a big advantage over your competitors.

Web forums

Step 6 recommended that you not set up private forums because of the resources required to manage the various risks involved in forums. However, if you make the forums private and available only to customers you reduce the dangers substantially.

Private forums are an excellent tool for customer service and feedback, as they are the first place your customers will go online to ask about problems or difficulties they are having. By being active in monitoring and open in discussing any issues, you help build trust and confidence with your customer base.

Old-fashioned media

Since a customer may have a few hundred unread messages in their inbox, it's not unusual to find postcards, letters and phone calls work well too. We shouldn't forget the older ways of doing business. Not only are these still valid today, if anything they are enhanced by the newer media tools.

Sending letters or postcards is a lot more expensive than email, so it's best to reserve this for your top customers. Like everything in business, the Pareto Rule applies: 20 per cent of customers generate 80 per cent of your turnover and profits. So it's worthwhile giving those customers a little more love than the others.

Birthday and Christmas cards along with gifts or letters with special offers and early notice of new products are all ways of retaining the best of your client base. Many long-established businesses, particularly in hospitality, are very good at this and have survived decades by understanding the importance of making their best customers feel special. Airline frequent flier programs are a great example of how to look after the big spenders.

Coupon offers

In early 2011 there was a mania for group buying programs, through which businesses give out coupons for internet sales. Companies offered anything from 20 per cent to 80 per cent off the list price of their products.

One of the big dangers with this customer acquisition strategy is that you can upset your existing clients, so it's worthwhile, through social media or email or direct mail channels, to offer something similar to your existing, loyal customers.

Like social media, the group buying strategy is relatively new—albeit based on deep discounting and coupons, which are probably two of the oldest business ideas going—so it's worth experimenting to see how you can merge the various marketing and customer engagement possibilities to get a great result for your business.

Conclusion

The internet's biggest effect on business is probably how the web has empowered customers. They are able to go online and research or complain about our services. We need to be there so we can deal with them on their own terms.

The next chapter takes us into step 7 of creating an online presence for your business, where the focus will be on staying up to date and relevant, and finally looking at how the Net will develop in the future and what that might mean for your business.

Checklist

> ➤ Are you checking your websites and social media pages at least daily in case any issues have arisen?

> ➤ How often are you contacting customers?

> ➤ Do you collect your customers' email addresses efficiently?

> ➤ Have you ensured that everyone on your email list has consented to receive emails from you?

> ➤ Are you collecting material for a regular newsletter?

> ➤ Do your emails have an easy unsubscribe feature?

> ➤ Can your accounting software or customer relationship management program identify your most valuable customers?

Step 7

Staying relevant

Chapter 18
Ongoing maintenance

No matter how good your websites or how clever your use of social media, the biggest challenge for everybody on the internet is staying up to date and relevant: the web loves action and visitors want useful and current information. A stale, outdated website is a very poor image for a business.

While you can get away with a brochure-ware site — a web page that is just an electronic version of a business brochure — that just states your business, address and opening hours, if you want maximum value from your website you need to be telling the world what you're doing now. Fresh, regularly updated sites attract the attention of search engines, and if visitors know there will be something new on your site on a regular basis, they are more likely to return regularly. More importantly, people checking your business out notice how up to date the site is: a website that has new and relevant information gives the impression that the business is dynamic and involved.

What you should put on the site varies according to the nature of your business and your industry. It's worth tapping into larger trends, such as the news of the day and events, along with news from within your own business, and posting the things your customers want to hear and read about in your industry.

Where should you be updating?

The obvious answer to this question is that you should be updating your data everywhere the business has a web presence: Twitter, Facebook, Local Search and—most importantly—your website. To update on every platform is going to be time consuming, and will increase the opportunities to make mistakes when copying content between the services.

Luckily, you can connect most services into the various social media accounts. For example, LinkedIn and Facebook have these functions built in if you are using the standard blogging platforms, such as Blogger or Wordpress, as we discussed in steps 1 and 6.

Facebook is particularly easy to update. In the 'Notes' application, which you can find by typing 'notes' into the search box at the top, you can link to a web page feed through the 'Import a blog' link on the right-hand side of your main Facebook profile. Clicking on that link will take you to a screen where your site feed can be entered, which will automatically post to your Facebook page anything new you add to your website.

While Facebook has a basic built-in tool to run these services, LinkedIn and Twitter have various plug-in or add-on programs that do the same thing. The easiest way to update material to these sites is to install a plug-in application on your website, which will automatically feed updates to your social media platforms.

Of course, you need to have things worth updating your website and social media feeds. Luckily this isn't as difficult or daunting as it sounds. In business heaps of things are changing around us every day: in fact, it can be harder to choose what not to update.

Cyclical information

Every industry has its own big days: office supplies during the back to school period, hairdressers and hatmakers before Melbourne Cup; and restaurants during the Christmas party season are just three examples. The Australian Newsagency Blog's football tipping competition is another example, shown in figure 18.1.

Figure 18.1: Australian Newsagency Blog football tipping

It's a great idea to put information on your website at the time people are making those bookings or looking for ideas; this establishes you and your business as leaders in that part of the industry, which in turn is going to attract more visitors and customers.

Being an industry thought leader also means the media are going to come to you. Journalists now go to the web first to find suitable experts to quote on issues in the news. If your website comes up first in a search, then you will be called on to be an expert, further increasing your reputation with customers and prospective customers.

Current events

Responding to news that affects your business is also a good way of being topical. For a plumber, the local water authorities' declaring a drought may be a good way to publicise water-saving tips and how a new toilet cistern or water tank can help. Similarly, the collapse of an investment company might be a good opportunity for a financial planner to put up a topical post.

One important thing to keep in mind when updating your website to deal with topical issues is that you should use some judgment. Don't make light of people's misfortunes and never, ever make an opportunistic post over a tragedy or disaster, as this can genuinely damage your business.

New products

Whenever you launch a new product, make sure it's added to the front page of your website. This is news you want to be proud and loud about, so let the world know what you are doing. When announcing new products, make sure the details, pricing and pictures are correct across all the channels you use, with links back to the website, to ensure you're driving the maximum amount of traffic into your site.

New products are one of the best ways to get a buzz happening around your business, so it's great to make a splash on your site and push the message out through social media.

Special offers and coupons

While the coupon mania thrives, we shouldn't forget many of the features are built into Google Places and True Local. Changing your offers regularly—for instance, having a two-for-one deal this month and a 10 per cent discount offer next month—is a good way to keep the coupons on your site ticking over.

Anything on the coupon sites should also be reflected in the home page of your website, which in turn should feed into the other marketing channels. This helps all of your sites work better.

Images

Web-surfers and the search engines they rely on love images, so get some on your site and update them regularly. Step 5 emphasised the importance of having well-named images on your site so the web spiders know what they are looking at. This also applies to anything new you put up on your website.

Showing new products and services is a great reason to add new images to your website. Adding a photo—with a good descriptive name—of that new valve, hairstyle or gourmet pizza will improve your search engine rankings and the look of your website, so don't neglect the pictures.

The stock photo dilemma

One of the ongoing debates in the webmaster and marketing world is the use of stock photos—the images you can buy from agencies rather than taking your own pictures.

Taking photos is a skill and amateur, poorly lit, photos don't work well on business websites. Calling in the professionals is really the only option for anyone wanting a high-quality website. The trouble is that a professional photographer can be expensive, and many small business don't want to use one. Even bigger companies baulk at the cost of having hundreds of photos taken for their product lines.

An answer to this is the stock photo. You simply pay to use images from a library of standard photos. It's quick and usually cheaper than hiring in a photographer.

Saying *usually cheaper* is important, as there are a few traps in buying stock photographs. The biggest catch is the licensing conditions, as most stock photographs are licensed for certain uses, so putting an image on a website or in a brochure may have different restrictions to using it in an ebook or advertising campaign. Licensees (that's you, if you pay for the use of a photo) also find they can be charged for each use of the image, so there are separate fees each time the picture appears on a site or brochure. Again these costs can add up quickly.

Those licensing fees can easily increase your costs beyond what a photographer would charge. And if others use the same stock photos as you do, the same pretty girl might appear all over the world on all manner of sites.

For smaller businesses, stock photos are good for general pictures. But if you're after a unique look or you need a lot of photos, a good professional photographer can be a good investment.

Personal opinions

Your views matter and putting them out in the marketplace is a good way of creating buzz. If you have a view on the new opening hours or how an interest rate change will affect your business, then it is definitely worthwhile putting it out there.

Being open and frank will get visitors engaged and sharing their stories and views with you. If you are going to do this, you need to be prepared to take some flack and deal with criticism as well. As discussed in step 2, there are many people who think the semi-anonymous nature of the internet allows them to be rude, so understand you have to deal with that.

While it's a bad move to delete criticisms of you, it is important that you keep control of the comments in your personal blog. Anything that is getting too heated, defamatory or downright illegal can't be tolerated. All the blog platforms include an option for you to approve comments before they are published, and it's essential you turn this feature on.

Guest posters

Sharing the love with other bloggers and websites is another excellent way of attracting visitors to your site, as your guest's regular visitors will tend to come to you as well. By cross-promoting each other's businesses and ideas, you can also grow your profile with people who normally wouldn't be your customers.

Choosing someone in a complementary industry, say an accountant posting on a lawyer's blog or a builder posting on a home improvement website, adds value for the website's readers and makes them aware of the other business's services.

Dealing with the haters

Unfortunately we also have to deal with the people who aren't happy with our views and ideas. So be prepared for some critics or—as internet slang says—the haters. Many of the critics are people with a good point to make, some of whom struggle to make those points in an articulate way. You can learn from them in ways that can improve both your website and business. Others are simply mad, and unfortunately the fallacy that you're anonymous on the internet only encourages them.

When someone who appears to be irrational confronts you online, it's best not to engage. If their comments aren't offensive or libellous, then the best course of action is to simply leave the posts up and block them from making further comments. Deleting their comments will actually provoke them, and leaving them up only confirms to your sensible followers that the poster is out of line.

Conclusion

Keeping your site up to date is an important part of your business's credibility in both the online and offline worlds. It's worthwhile spending a few hours a month making sure it reflects what's going on in your market and industry.

Both the online and offline worlds are changing rapidly and you need to adapt and move with them as well as keep your customers abreast with changes in your industry. Keeping engaged and keeping your sites up to date will make that a simpler process. Chapter 19 looks at some of the new trends online and how they might affect your business.

Checklist

➤ Are your updates relevant to your business and customers?

➤ Are you making sure updates appear on your website home page?

➤ Are you announcing all new products on the home page of your website?

➤ Can you create a new offer every month?

➤ Have you thought about building an annual calendar around important industry events?

➤ Are you watching your sites and ensuring all comments are moderated?

➤ Have you thought of ways you can be a thought leader in your industry?

Chapter 19

Future opportunities

We're at the beginning of a time of great change in the online world — and the rate is accelerating rapidly. The internet itself developed into what we know today in the 1980s and 1990s. Until the mid 1990s, mobile phones were the preserve of the rich, and smart phones were unthought of; the world wide web itself only came into being in 1993. Because all of these technologies are relatively new, we're all still exploring the opportunities these methods and tools offer for business. It also means that few people are really experts in these fields.

As our knowledge of these tools and their effects on our business and customers grows, we will get better at using them. For now, we're playing at the edge of these opportunities. Nonetheless, there are clear trends developing that we need to watch.

The SoLoMo revolution

One trend that is developing now is the social local mobile (SoLoMo) revolution, in which our customers are using mobile phones to find local businesses with the help of their social networks. This is dramatically changing the way we advertise and position our businesses.

It's also a great opportunity for small business, as most big corporations are also struggling to understand this fundamental change in doing business and in many ways are more threatened by it than the smaller end of town. The centralised nature of most corporations means they can't react on a local level, and the homogenised nature of their products makes it difficult for them to offer a unique product that energises social networks.

Many local and mobile platforms are getting their information from services such as Google Places and True Local, which is why this book has talked a lot about getting listings in these services right. As we see more customers moving to smart phones, and devices like GPS systems incorporating search functions, we will see local services becoming more important.

Quality of data is an important issue for all of us, and we have to make sure that data on our business is correct. The web now has a horrible habit of allowing misinformation to spread, so by ensuring the details about our business online are correct and entered into the key listing services, we make sure the customers we want can find us.

Online commerce

While the shop front will never go away, as many customers prefer a physical store and some products are best sold that way, the move to online retail is increasing and shoppers are showing they appreciate the convenience and cost savings. Right now there are a few quirks and risks in setting up and accepting online payments and e-commerce, but processing is getting cheaper and easier, and the payment systems are getting better at fraud protection and prevention.

A big advantage with online payments is that your own staff can use them. So a plumber, courier or bookkeeper equipped with a smart phone and their own online payments gateway can accept customer payments while at a client's premises, reducing costs and bad debts.

Over time, most business are going to find an online payment gateway is essential, as other businesses and consumers expect it. The good news is that, with cloud computing, we can expect point of sales systems to move onto the Net and integrate the functions we now get in services such as eWay and PayPal.

Cloud computing

The return to the old-fashioned way of running computers — relatively dumb terminals connected to supercomputers, or in today's case super smart networks of cloud computers — opens up massive opportunities for small and startup businesses. With the technologies available in the cloud, we don't have to make massive investments in computer hardware and programs: instead we can pay as we go and reduce capital costs. Given that most cloud services can run on basic machines, this also reduces the replacement cycle, which saw us replacing computers every five years, or even more frequently.

Cloud computing also ties into the trend towards mobile computing, as the basic assumption of most services is that services will run on any device that can operate a web browser. This mean technology can follow us anywhere we have internet access.

Augmented reality

Bringing together the various technologies built into smart phones, such as GPS receivers, cameras and internet connections, has given rise to augmented reality applications, which can take a photo or video of a place and then add information pulled from the internet. A typical example of augmented reality is an application by ING Bank in the Netherlands that allows you to find nearby branches by opening the program and pointing your phone at a building or landmark—the software recognises your location and displays all of the bank's nearby outlets.

One great augmented reality application for the iPhone is a service called Layar, which takes the features in the phone and allows developers to create their own layers of information on top, so that restaurants, places of interest and pretty well anything you may be interested in can be displayed.

These services are all powered by local search, so the location and details of services, products and opening hours are all being taken from the listings available. It's another reason why businesses need to be listed in local directories.

Social media

While Facebook is the great tool of the moment, things are developing quickly, as we see the different platforms creating new alliances and products, and moving into areas such as payment systems and local search.

Social media offers some really interesting opportunities in customer support, employee engagement and marketing (see steps 1 and 6). For any business prepared to think outside the box, there's great potential for getting a jump on the rest of the market.

Many businesses are going to find social media offers one of the best opportunities to win new customers and build great brands. The nature of tools such as Twitter and Facebook—and the many that haven't been invented yet—allows a business to create a loyal band of followers.

It's going to be worthwhile watching what happens in the social media industry as new services are released. It's quite clear that we have only scratched the surface of this technology, and the community aspects of social media are radically changing how our customers think and interact with both big and small brands.

The customer

The rise of the internet means one thing is clear: the customer is king again. Not only does the web give the consumer more information about the quality and price of what's available, but we're now also able to deliver products quickly anywhere in the world. It means our competition is no longer the guy on the next corner or in the next suburb—they could just as easily be on the other side of the world.

We have to accept that our mistakes are going to be magnified when we are online and engaged with the social media. And we have to concentrate more on keeping customers happy when we make errors. In many ways that's good, because this will give the advantage back to smaller, more client-focused businesses at the expense of larger, more slow-moving, bureaucratic corporations.

Staff

Increasingly we will use the web to recruit and retain staff. Whether we like it or not, they are going to be on Facebook and LinkedIn comparing notes about their employers and which are the best places to work. We're going to have to learn how to use these tools and engage with staff, who increasingly consider these services essential to their business lives.

Conclusion

All of this shows that we're in a period of change and many organisations that grew big in the twentieth century are going to struggle in this new world. This is a time of great opportunity for the agile, flexible business. In many ways this book has been about positioning your business to look towards the future. It's going to be a wild ride, so strap yourself in and enjoy it!

Checklist

➤ Are you keeping up to date with how your customers and staff are using technology and how the online world is changing?

➤ Are you ready to experiment?

➤ Are you ready to grab opportunities when they arise?

➤ Are you watching for trends and hot new products?

➤ Are you taking care not to block new tools from your business?

➤ Are you ready to enjoy the ride?

➤ And never forget, business is about the customer.

Appendix A

Getting Australian Business Online

At the time of writing, Google and MYOB launched their Getting Australian Business Online (GABO) service. GABO offers a free domain registration, a basic website and some of the simpler Google Places functions to any registered Australian business. This appendix looks at how GABO can help your business, the steps for setting it up and where you'll have to apply the ideas in this book to any GABO-based website.

Getting Australian Business Online explained

Around half of Australian businesses don't have a web presence. To overcome this, Google and MYOB now offer a free service for small businesses that provides an internet name, website and basic service (see figure A1). This service doesn't suit every business and is limited to the first 50 000 businesses who apply. If you are interested, check the *eBusiness* website at <www.ebusinessbook.com.au> to see if the service is still available.

Figure A1: Getting Australia Business Online

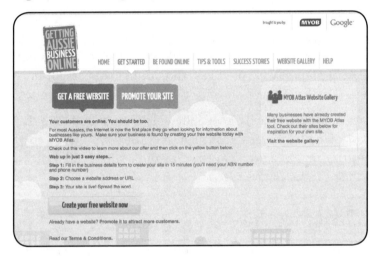

Is it for you?

GABO is a really basic product. It aims to get a business online quickly, so if you want a more sophisticated or a flexible presence it may not work for you.

An important thing to consider is that GABO sites have no online selling facilities beyond a contact phone number and email and street addresses. There is no way to integrate e-commerce features and any links, HTML coding and other features will be stripped out of the site. These sites are really only useful for the most basic online needs.

The service is aimed at small businesses that don't have the time, money or skills to set up and maintain a website. This is something that we hope this book has shown most people can do in seven easy steps.

What you get

The key attraction is the free domain name (the bit that goes after the www., such as netsmarts.com.au in the address <www.netsmarts.com.au>), which saves about $20 per year (see step 2).

You will also receive a very basic website where you can post upcoming events, use a gallery to upload images and descriptions of your products, and document pages for price lists, and have a map showing the location of your premises.

Overall you get the basics required in a website and little else. For many businesses, that might be just what they need at a price much lower than the cost of classified ads in local papers or the Yellow Pages.

The downside

The downside of the GABO product is that you won't get a flashy website — it will be a very basic template without much to see. You won't get an email address to go with the free domain name, so you will have to use your internet service provider's address. Producing an address like mylocalshop@ bigpond.com.au isn't a good look, as you business will look like a smaller outfit than you might like.

GABO websites are intended for small businesses that tend not to have created an online presence because they haven't had the time, money or skills to set up a website. Because these are simple sites, compromises have been made, so you won't get all the features offered by services such as Blogger, Weebly or Wordpress (see step 1).

The service is free for only the first year; after that it is charged at a rate of $5 a month and the domain name has to be renewed after two years for $30. Overall those charges aren't excessive, but as you have seen from step 2 in this book, there are better value options.

Setting up

The setting-up process is straightforward, albeit a little long winded. You need to log into the service either with a Google account or with Facebook, LinkedIn or Twitter. I recommend setting up through your Google account.

Once you have logged in (see figure A2), you will be prompted to fill in your business details. The first field is your Australian business number (ABN), and this will be checked against the Australian Business Number Registry to verify the name, and create an account with the MYOB service in the name listed in the register (see figure A3, overleaf).

Figure A2: login screen for Getting Australian Business Online

The screen called *Adding your contact details* is important, as they are the details customers will see when they visit your website. Tick the 'Find us' box if you want the address to appear on the website; if you're a home-based or mobile business you may not want to do this.

Figure A3: fill in your business details

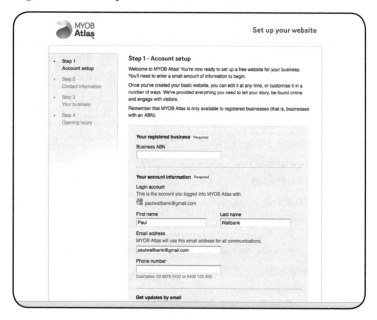

Your contact details are the most important part of this service. The descriptions you enter here will become the text of your website, which is what the search engines will look for. Remember that the keywords are what your customers will search for, as described in step 5. Spending a few hours on your research and rewriting your text will pay big dividends.

Describing your business is the key screen where you get to add the vital details that will appear on the site and be indexed by Google. The 'Title' field at the top should describe your business in a simple way—such as 'Fred's Pie Shop in Maroubra' or 'Sally's Dog-Walking, Sunshine Coast'—as this is one of the key search fields.

The byline, or website tagline, below 'Title' is important, too, because it will appear in the search results for your business. It should add a bit more detail to the title field: for instance, 'Tasty hot pies and delicious cakes and pastries' or 'Exercise for your pet'.

Probably the most important of all these essential fields is the company description (see figure A4). The field is limited to 500 characters, so you can be fairly descriptive but you can't write a novel. Make sure the keywords for search engines appear in that description.

Figure A4: your contact information

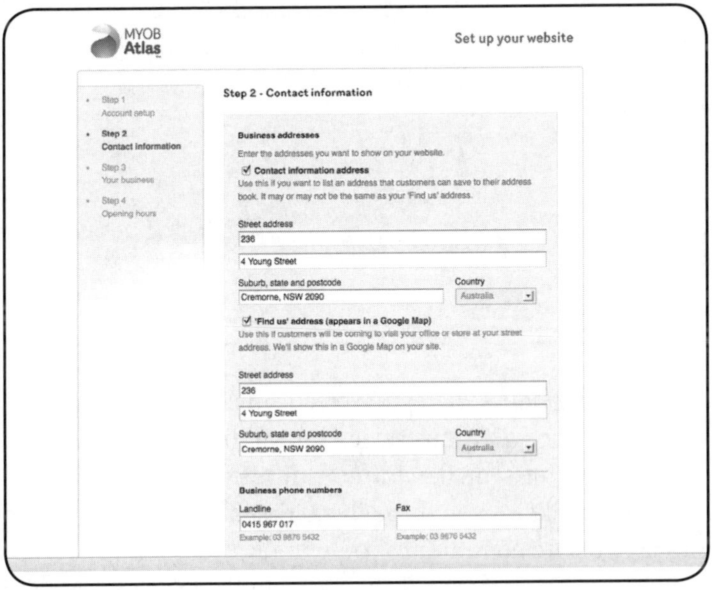

Below the descriptions, you can add a logo or banner (a longer image usually including your logo and business name) to the screen. As discussed in step 5, it helps to give all images, including any banners, a descriptive name such as 'Sallys_ sunshine_coast_dog_walking.jpg' to help the search engines.

If you don't have a banner image available, choose 'Add this later' and go on to the next screen.

Opening hours aren't a mandatory field (see figure A5), but they do help in searches because the search engines love you more if there's more detail in your information. Add something into the comment that picks up a couple of your keywords.

Figure A5: opening hours

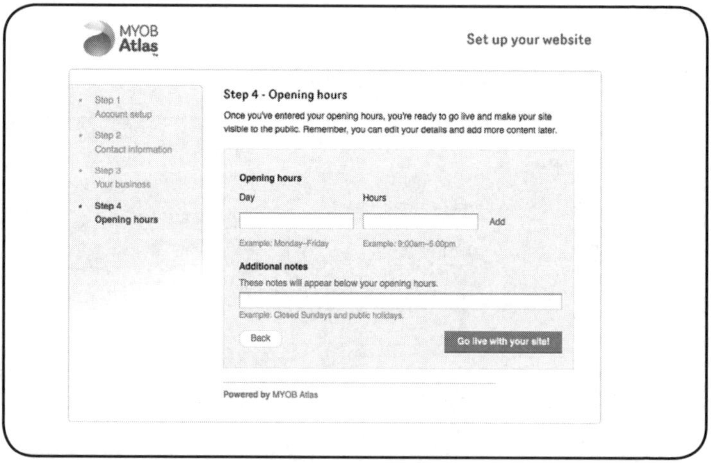

The opening hours dialogue screen finishes the first part of the setup process. At this stage you will have a website setup with the address in the form yourbusiness.myob.net. The next stage will take you through the domain name registration process. Before continuing, you will receive a summary page explaining the elements of the page you have just set up and how you can change them.

Some useful resources are linked at the bottom of the *Welcome* screen (see figure A6), marked as 'Free education resources from Google' and 'Take a peek at some other small business websites powered by MYOB Atlas'. Both of these are good reference documents to give you some ideas about what to include on your page.

Figure A6: welcome to the Atlas website screen

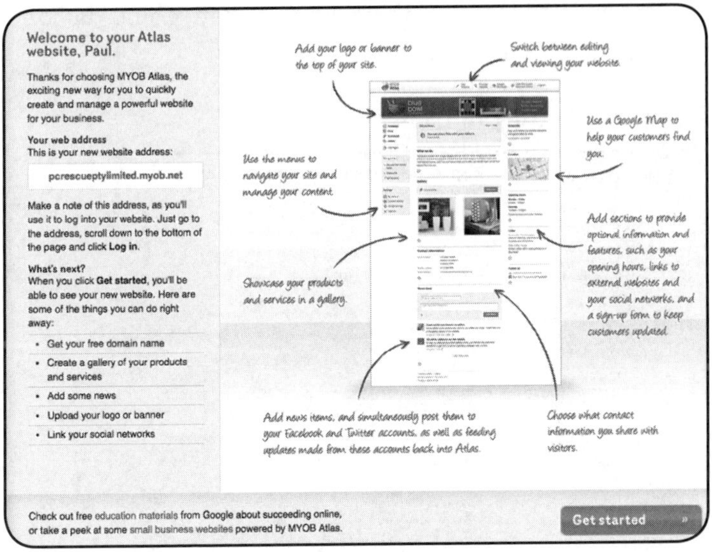

Claiming your free domain

The following screens take you through the process of claiming the free domain. The details you enter here will be the ones registered against your ownership of the internet name as we described in step 2, so it's important to make sure these are correct to avoid problems down the track.

Type the domain name you want into the 'Find your domain name' box, and the site will automatically check it (see figure A7, overleaf). Be careful with the domain name suggested by the service that appears as it will probably contain hyphens, which are generally bad for domain names.

If the name you want isn't available, then follow the guidelines given in step 2 for creating a name as close as possible to your business name. You may want to add a word like 'shop', 'service' or 'store' to the end of the name or, if you're a local service like a plumber or shop, you could add the suburb to the address to make it unique; for instance, Joe's plumbers in Croydon could become joescroydonplumbers.com.au.

Figure A7: setting up your domain name

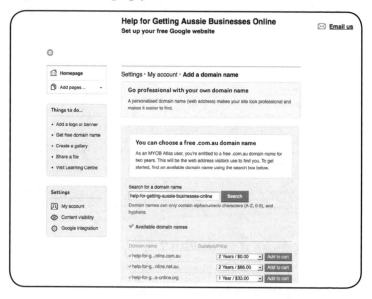

At the bottom of the page the price of the domain will be shown. For the .com.au domain the cost will be shown as $0, indicating there's no charge. Below that will be other options, such as .net.au and .org domains, which have charges attached. For most businesses these aren't necessary, particularly for those whose needs are met by this basic service.

The *Domain registration confirmation* page appears with the address details that were filled in earlier. These cannot be changed. Because of the rules around registration of Australian domain names, it's necessary to click the 'Domain Name

Eligibility' button to confirm that you believe you qualify for the domain name.

At the end of the process you will be taken to your completed site. The little cog icons will take you to the settings for each element and you can modify, add and remove functions from there.

Keep in mind the domain you have applied for won't take effect immediately: it normally takes a day for it to be processed by MYOB and for it to be added into the DNS, which was described in step 2, but it should be running within 48 hours. In the meantime, add the domain name to the local and search engine registrations described in step 1.

Further customisations

On the *Your business* page, GABO has the feature for adding links to your Twitter and Facebook accounts that will automatically update your feeds with any changes you make to your page. This is a good idea, as described in steps 1 and 6. These updates will help the search engines find you and, if your customers find your updates interesting, they will share your news with their social media followers.

At the end of the signup process you will also be directed to the Google Places and Adwords signups; follow the Places signup as described in step 1. Adwords, which was described in step 5, will give you a taste of online advertising aided by the free vouchers Google usually offers online or through various promotions.

Other services

While GABO should list your site with Google's search engine automatically, don't take any chances, and still submit it yourself with the services described in steps 1 and 4. While you might not immediately have the domain name available while it's being processed, it is worthwhile making sure the site is in the queue to be indexed by Google, Yahoo! and Bing.

The listing in Google Places shouldn't be taken for granted either, so you should set up a full profile there, making sure all the details you have entered, including photos and documents, are attached as well. Complete a True Local profile for the business as well (see step 1).

Upgrading

There is no real upgrade path with the GABO websites. The proprietary nature of the MYOB Atlas platform means it doesn't plug into the major platforms described in step 3, so if your business needs outgrow the basic site, you will have to re-enter the information. Fortunately, that's not too great a problem, as the information itself is fairly basic, so there isn't much work involved in re-creating it. Given that GABO doesn't support links, plug-ins or website features, included in all but the most basic websites, a GABO site is going to require an upgrade for most businesses anyway.

GABO sites are useful for the smaller business wanting a really basic website, but many other options that offer much more flexibility for less than $100 a year are available.

Appendix B

Choosing a consultant

As much as we would like to think we can do everything ourselves, the truth is we can't. Even the biggest organisations don't always have the right skills for a task that needs to be done. Enter the consultant.

Consultants have had bad press in recent years due to a combination of misunderstandings and misuse by big and small organisations. Ideally the consulting company will bring a fresh set of eyes and skills to projects that are not central to the daily running of your business. So how do you go about choosing a consultant?

Do they show up on time?

If a consultant is unreliable when they are chasing your work, what makes you think they will be any better when you hire them? If you're hounding them for quotes and proposals, then you have to wonder if they are really capable of doing the job. The time required to reply to an enquiry is a good indicator that should help you whittle down the long list into a short list.

The internet is your friend

An experienced consultant will have a digital footprint, and have articles, white papers, blogs and a website online. These are a good guide to the areas the consultant is an expert in. For consulting firms, white papers, which discuss industry issues in depth, can be powerful marketing tools to show off their expertise.

Read their public utterances

Reading online posts will dig up that consultant's, or their staff's, views on the market and the different solutions they have come up with. Comments on other people's sites by the firm's principals and employees is a great way to see how deep their expertise is and how well they are regarded in the industry. This is also a good way to check that their values align with yours.

Something that catches out a lot of the self-proclaimed social media experts and marketing people is that they often show their talk of trust and openness is little more than talk. If a consultant's tweets, comments or Facebook wall posts are at odds with what they are telling you, then that is a danger sign.

Check references

The consultant's website will cite the clients they have worked for. Pick up the phone and talk to the clients to find out if the consultant really did this work? How effective were they?

If your consultant is an individual, part of that digital footprint is social media. Tools like LinkedIn and Facebook help for checking references as well. LinkedIn, especially, has a recommendations section that is a handy quick reference checker. Don't be shy about contacting those people to check the truth of the recommendations posted.

Understand their biases

We all have biases towards certain solutions. As the US industrial psychologist Abraham Maslow said, 'When all you own is a hammer, every problem starts looking like a nail.' In technology this is particularly pronounced, as consulting firms small and large have made a substantial investment in one platform or another. This isn't a bad thing, but keep their biases in mind and ask questions about why they are proposing a certain course of action over alternatives.

Know their expertise

The whole point of hiring a consultant is for them to do a task you aren't familiar with. If you ask the consultant to do something outside their immediate area of expertise, then your fees are paying for them to train in a new area. Good for them—but not for you.

Are they too agreeable?

If the consultant agrees with you all the time, then there's little point in hiring them except for self-validation. A good consultant will be prepared to gently steer you away from silly decisions. On the other hand, a consultant who screams at you or puts down your staff's views is best let go.

Trust your instincts

If something about a particular proposal, individual or organisation doesn't work for you, then look elsewhere. If you're uncomfortable before signing an agreement, imagine how you will feel when the invoices start arriving.

Price should not be the factor

Choosing a consultant purely on cost is risky. There are real traps in going for the cheapest option. Invariably, cheaper and less experienced consultants will require more handholding, which will make demands on your management time.

A good consultant is worth their weight in gold and finding one is a great help for your business. A little due diligence through the hiring process makes sure you get the person right for your needs.

Jargon buster

A/B Testing   The process of testing different website designs to see what works best.

add-ons   *see* Plug-ins.

alt tags   These describe what is in a web link, image or video so that a search engine or accessibility program can understand the content.

CAPTCHA   A little program built into websites that asks you to enter a nonsense word or two in an attempt to prove you're human and not a piece of software.

CMS (content management system)   A computer program or web service that manages the information you put on your website. CMS can also refer to contact management service for tracking your contacts.

CName (canonical name)   A setting that tells computers where your website can be found on the internet.

CPC (cost per click)   A method of billing online advertisers.

dedicated hosting   This occurs when an organisation has one machine and internet address dedicated to their Net presence and not shared with anyone else.

domain   The name of site on the internet.

DNS (Domain Name Service)   This translates human names, such as Google.com, into machine-readable internet protocol addresses.

feed   The information from a website sent to another site. You can feed your Twitter posts to Facebook so they appear in both places.

host   The computer, known as a server, that makes information available to other computers.

hosting   A service — usually consisting of a big company with lots of computers — that provides the server space for websites.

HTML (hypertext markup language)   The basic language of web page design.

ICANN (Internet Committee on Assigned Names)   The organisation responsible for keeping track of internet names.

indexing/indexed   The listing of website details and content by search engines.

IP (internet protocol)   The language computers use to talk across the internet.

ISP Internet Service Provider   The organisation that connects you to the internet

jpg (joint picture group)   A common image format standard that is popular on the web.

name servers   The name of a web or email server.

PHP (personal home page)   A basic scripting language that runs many internet services.

plug-ins   Mini-programs that run on websites and add special functions, such as showing advertisements, calendars or mailing list signups.

registrar   The organisation that registers an internet name.

RSS (really simple syndication)   A standard for sharing information from a website. *See also* Feeds.

SEO (search engine optimisation)   Techniques for making a website more visible to web search engines such as Google and Microsoft Bing.

server   A computer that gives out information to other computers.

Shared hosting   Cheap internet hosting that puts a number of customers on the same computer and internet connection.

SLA (service level agreement)   An agreement that a provider will give you a certain level of service.

spider   The software used by search engines to gather information on websites.

TLD (top level domain)   The part of a website address that comes at the end of a name, after the dot, such as .com, .gov, .org, .com.au and govt.nz

uptime   How long a service runs without shutting down.

URL (universal resource locator)   The techie name for a web address.

webserver   A computer that makes a website available to the internet.

widgets.   *see* Plug-ins.

Index